PRESS FOR ACTION

Science
Sound, Light and Space

Bob Haywood
Michael Pearce

Folens Publishers

Sound, Light and Space

Folens
COPYMASTER

Folens books are protected by international copyright laws. All rights reserved. The copyright of all materials in this book, except where otherwise stated, remains the property of the publisher and author(s). No part of this publication may be reproduced, stored in a retrieval system, or transmitted, in any form or by any means, for whatever purpose, without the written permission of Folens Limited.

Folens do allow photocopying of selected pages of this publication for educational use, providing that this use is within the confines of the purchasing institution. You may make as many copies as you require for classroom use of the pages so marked.

This resource may be used in a variety of ways; however, it is not intended that teachers or students should write directly into the book itself.

© 1991 Folens Limited, on behalf of the authors.

First published 1991 by Folens Limited, Albert House, Apex Business Centre, Boscombe Road, Dunstable LU5 4RL, England.

ISBN 1 85276150-4

Illustration by Turner's, Dunstable and Pat Murray.

Printed in Great Britain by Ashford Colour Press.

Contents

Introduction	4
Reference Grid	5
Rainbows and Coloured Lights	6 - 7
Slide Projectors	8 - 9
Light in Our Eyes	10 - 11
Mirror, Mirror on the Wall	12 - 13
Keeping an Image	14 - 15
Eyesight Problems	16 - 17
Light Law	18 - 19
Back-to-Front Reflection	20 - 21
All Done with Mirrors	22 - 23
Moving Pictures	24 - 26
The Electromagnetic Spectrum	27
Waves All Around	28 - 29
Hear Ear!	30 - 31
Sound Survey	32 - 33
Noise or Music?	34 - 36
Speed of Sound	37
History of Space Flight	38 - 39
Moon Matters	40 - 41
Twinkle, Twinkle Little Star	42 - 43
Seeing Stars!	44 - 45
Our Solar System	46
Teachers' Notes	47 - 48

Introduction

SCIENCE IN THE NATIONAL CURRICULUM

This book is one in a series written with the purpose of providing a variety of photocopiable activities for students following the National Curriculum Programme of Study at Key Stage 3. Each activity has been designed to help students develop some of the appropriate processes, skills and concepts in order to meet the demands of the Attainment Targets.

The limited space available has meant that we have had to be selective in our choice of activities. We have therefore not been able to provide activities to match all the Statements of Attainment contained within levels 3 - 7 of the Attainment Targets.

We have tried to provide material which is consistent with our view that a "balanced approach" to the National Curriculum is more desirable. By a balanced approach, we mean that students should experience their science in a challenging way which carefully balances a process-led approach to experimentation and evidence with a planned sequence of activities that assists concept formation and development. When these are presented to students in contexts which they see as interesting and relevant to their lives and which encourage debate, they become more motivated to learn and begin to incorporate scientific views into their interpretations of the world. This view seems consistent with the aims and structure of the National Curriculum document. The emphasis given to exploration and investigation, both in the relevant Programme of Study and the associated assessment weighting, ought to permeate the teaching and learning of science at this stage in a thoroughly integrated fashion. Similarly, allowing students to discuss, reflect upon and evaluate their learning, not only enables concept formation and modification, but is consistent with an understanding of the nature of science outlined in the National Curriculum.

Attainment Target 1 (Scientific Investigation) has been restructured under four headings to provide a model which students can use to structure their experimental work. These headings are:

PLANNING

- identifying and controlling variables
- planning a fair test of a given problem
- planning a fair test of their own problem

PERFORMING AND RECORDING

- observing and measuring
- handling materials and apparatus safely

INTERPRETING

- inferring
- classifying
- making predictions
- forming generalised ideas

COMMUNICATING

- receiving information and instructions and reporting in a variety of forms

There are a number of component skills within many of the processes, such as "controlling variables" and "communicating". For example, in communicating the results of an experiment, students may employ their skills in writing a sequenced account, tabulating data and in graphicacy. Student performance in the Scientific Investigation Profile Component is to be assessed by matching the evidence from such activities against the indicated levels of attainment - a task which will require experience in interpretation. In **PRESS FOR ACTION: SCIENCE**, we have provided a resource which corresponds with the processes and component skills over the range of Attainment Levels for Key Stage 3.

The reference grid on Page 5 attempts to match the activities within the Press for Action: Science series to:

- processes within AT1 (Scientific Investigation), and
- the relevant Attainment Target(s)[*] and associated Level(s) of Attainment.

AT1	Scientific Investigation
AT2	Life and Living Processes
AT3	Materials and Their Properties
AT4	Physical Processes

[*]*Attainment Targets as defined in the NCC Consultative document, September 1991.*

© 1991 Folens Limited

Reference Grid

Living Things

Title of activity	Plan	Perf	Int	Com	AT 2	AT 3
Living Experiments	•		•		L3	
Woodlice and Fertiliser	•		•		L4	
Milk	•	•	•	•	L5	
Shukla's Sweets	•		•	•	L5	
Rats on a Diet			•	•	L6	
Pasteurisation			•	•	L5	
Seeds			•	•	L5	
Dead or Alive?					L3	
Animal Puzzles					L3/4	
Fossils					L4	
Crowkey					L4	
Coastal Food Web			•	•	L4/5	
Salt Marsh					L5/6	
Woodland Invertebrates			•	•	L6	
Marram Grass			•	•	L5/6	
All in Vein!					L4/5	
Broad Bean					L4	
Good Health!					L4/5	
Health Survey	•		•	•		
Organs					L4	
Alexis St. Martin			•	•	L5	
Hole in the Heart					L5/7	
That's What You Think!			•	•	L5	
Alison's Tomatoes			•	•	L4	
Ugly Bug Ball			•	•	L5/7	
Mint, Mice and Candles			•	•	L5	
Digit Person					L3	
Top Class Running			•	•	L5/6	
Stress			•	•	L5	
Car Pollution			•		L5	L4

Forces and Electricity

Title of activity	Plan	Perf	Int	Com	AT 3	AT 4
Measuring Forces	•		•	•		L4
Making Rocks			•	•	L6	
Measuring Friction			•			L4
Stopping a Car			•	•		L3/4
Effect of an Impact	•					L4
Bicycle Ride			•			L5
Measuring Speed			•			L5
Going Faster			•			L5
Fast Cars			•	•		L5/6
Work			•			L7
Energy Changers			•	•		L3
Conductors and Insulators	•			•		L7
Floating and Sinking	•			•		L3/6
Magnetic Fields				•		L1/6
Shorthand Circuits			•	•		L4
Putting Lights On	•		•			L4/5
Electric Currents			•			L4/5
Ammeters and Voltmeters				•		L6
Plug Safety		•				PoS
Using Electricity Safely				•		PoS
Electricity Costs			•	•		PoS
Magnets and Switches				•		L7
Logic Gates			•	•		L5
Analogue and Digital			•	•		L4/5
Electronic Codes				•		L5

Materials

Title of activity	Plan	Perf	Int	Com	AT 3
Kinking Straws	•		•	•	L4
Solid, Liquid or Gas?					L3/4/5
Chemical Reactions					L4/5
Material Spotters					L4/5
Thinking About Air			•		L5/6
Solubility Testing	•		•	•	L4
Biotechnology					L4/5/7
Separating Mixtures					L5
Donna's Crystals			•		L5
Cash for Cans					L4/5/6
Acid or Alkali?	•		•	•	L5
Melting and Boiling			•	•	L5
Copper Compounds	•		•	•	L5/6
Reaction Teasers					L6
Solution Mixers			•	•	L6
Dalton's Atomic Ideas				•	L5
Rate of Reaction			•	•	L7

Sound, Light and Space

Title of activity	Plan	Perf	Int	Com	AT 4
Rainbows and Coloured Lights			•		PoS
Slide Projectors			•	•	L3/4
Light in Our Eyes			•	•	L4
Mirror, Mirror on the Wall				•	L3/4
Keeping an Image					PoS
Eyesight Problems		•			PoS
Light Law			•		L3/4/5
Back-to-Front Reflection			•	•	L3/4/5
All done with Mirrors				•	L3/4
Moving Pictures				•	PoS
Waves All Around				•	L6
Hear Ear!				•	PoS
Sound Survey			•	•	L6
Noise or Music?			•	•	L6
Speed of Sound		•	•		PoS
History of Space Flight				•	PoS
Moon Matters				•	L3
Twinkle, Twinkle Little Star				•	L6
Seeing Stars!			•	•	L6
Our Solar System			•	•	L4/8

KEY:

Plan	=	Planning
Perf	=	Performing
Int	=	Interpreting
Com	=	Communicating

•	=	Activity supports this process
L	=	Levels of Attainment
L3/4	=	Opportunity to display skills and/or understanding at more than one level according to outcome.
PoS	=	Refer to Programme of Study

© 1991 Folens Limited

Rainbows and Coloured Lights

This activity will teach you about the mixture of coloured lights that together make up white light.

When people look at the world around them, they do not all see colours in the same way. Some people are partly **colour blind** and get red and green mixed up, but most people can clearly tell the difference between red and green lights.

A very small number of people see no colours at all and the world, to them, looks like the picture on a black and white television set. The eyes of people with normal sight are sensitive to a whole range of colours. When they look at a rainbow, they see all of the colours.

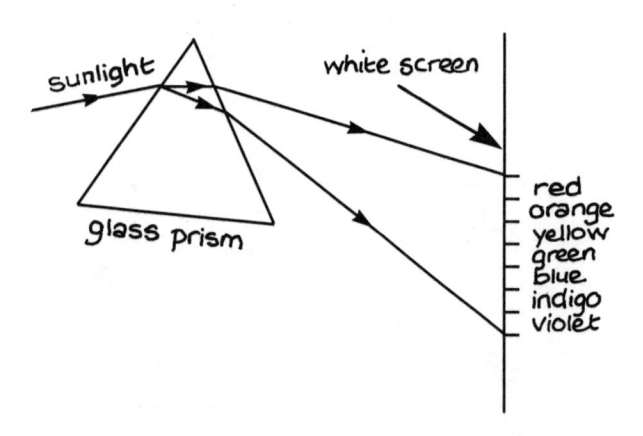

Light from the sun is 'white' - unless it passes through something which is transparent and 'coloured', or it reflects off the surface of an object containing a coloured pigment. White light is a mixture of all the colours we see when we look at a rainbow. These rainbow colours can be seen by passing sunlight through a **prism**.

In the rainbow, each raindrop behaves like a small prism splitting the white light into the spectrum of colours that we see. Because of what he observed from his experiments, Isaac Newton was the first person to infer that white light was made up of a mixture of lights of different colours.

The band of colour produced by the prism and seen in a rainbow is called a **spectrum**. The first person to carry out the prism experiment was Sir Isaac Newton in 1666.

When white light shines on to anything, some colours are **absorbed** and others are **reflected**.

If you look at a red car, only red light is reflected into your eyes. All the other colours which go to make white light are absorbed by the car.

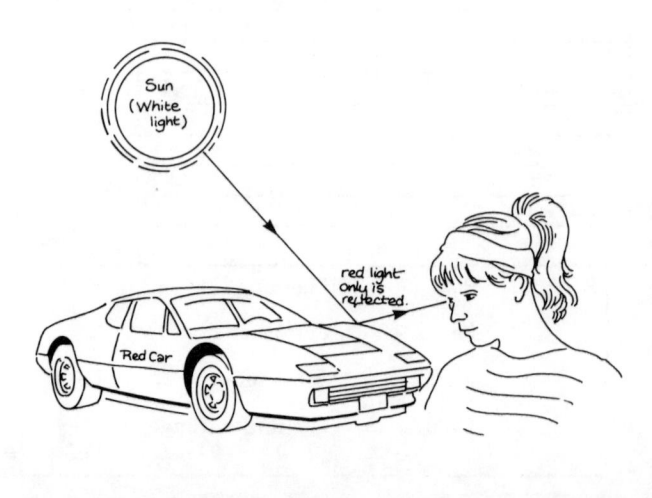

To a scientist, *red* is a **primary** colour, as are *green* and *blue*. None of these colours can be made from other colours in light.

If three spotlights, a *red* one, a *green* one and a *blue* one are shone on to a white screen and overlap, the following picture is seen:

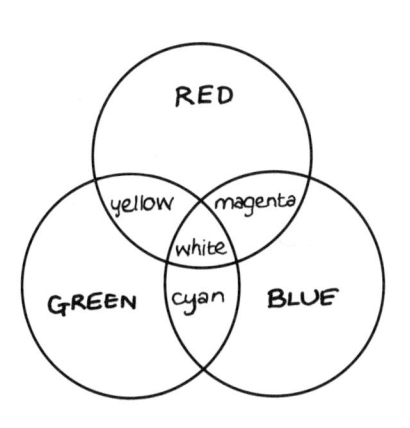

The colours in the overlap areas, yellow, magenta, and cyan are called **secondary** colours.

If two colours can join together to make white light, they are called **complementary** colours. Green and magenta are complementary colours.

If a dancer on stage is wearing a red dress and a green light shines on to her, the dress appears *black* because all the green light is absorbed and no light is reflected. If a yellow light shines on to the dress it appears red because the red part of the yellow is reflected.

If the dancer wore a yellow dress it would appear to be red in red light, green in green light and yellow in yellow light, as well as yellow in white light. However, if magenta, cyan or blue light shines on to the dress it appears to be black because no light is reflected from it.

Remember! Black is not a colour - it is the absence of any colour!

Task

1. Draw a circle of diameter 8cm on to thick white card. Split the circle into 3 equal parts (120° each). Colour in the sections *red*, *green*, and *blue*. Carefully cut out the disc and push a pencil through the centre so that it fits tightly. Spin the disc. What do you see? Why do you see it?

2. If a girl is wearing a magenta blouse, what colour would it appear to be in yellow light?

3. If a red car is parked under a yellow street lamp it appears to be black. Why?

4. If a sheet of white paper has blue crosses on it when looked at under white light, what will be seen if the same sheet of paper is looked at under blue light?

5. In white light, if a piece of white paper is looked at through a red filter, the paper looks red. What would the paper look like if a green filter was placed on top of the red filter?

Slide Projectors

This activity shows you how a slide projector works and some precautions to take when using one.

Mr. Gelsthorpe is going to talk to the new pupils at his school. He wants to use some slides to show the kind of lessons they will have and the sort of things they will be doing in them.

Mr. Mearns has set up a projector for him but has had to go off to do another job and has not had time to put the slides into the projector.

Mr. Gelsthorpe is not very good with equipment and the slides appear on the screen upside down and out of focus! Mr. Mearns comes to the rescue and decides that he needs to explain to Mr. Gelsthorpe how the projector works.

Mr. Mearns draws a diagram of the projector to help with his explanation.

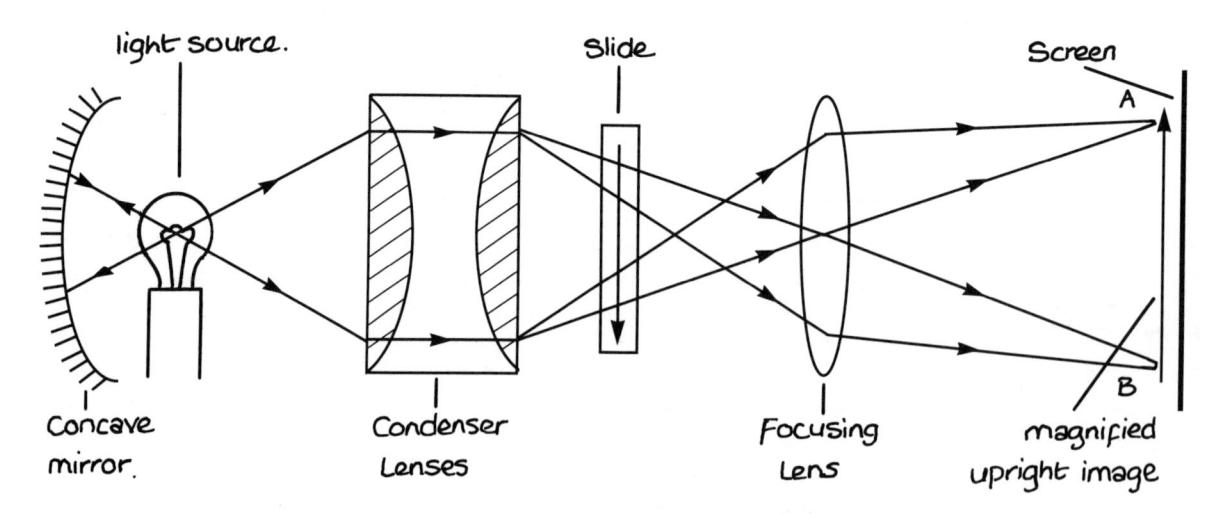

Diagram labels: light source, Slide, Screen, Concave mirror, Condenser Lenses, Focusing Lens, magnified upright image, A, B

'You need to get as much light on to the **slide** as you can so that a bright image is seen on the screen. This is done by using a powerful lamp of 500-600 watts. A curved **mirror** is put behind the lamp so that as much light as possible is reflected towards the slide. The **condenser lenses** collect and bend the light so that as much as possible passes through the slide. A **lens** at the front of the projector collects the light after it has passed through the slide and makes a bright image of it on the screen.

These projectors get very hot, so a cooling fan is fitted. The case has slots in it to let cool air in and the warm air out. A projector should never be moved just after it has been switched off! It should be left to cool down, or the lamp may be damaged.'

Task 1

1. The diagram below shows four slides. Which one is in the correct position to be placed in the projector to give an image that is the right way up and the right way round?

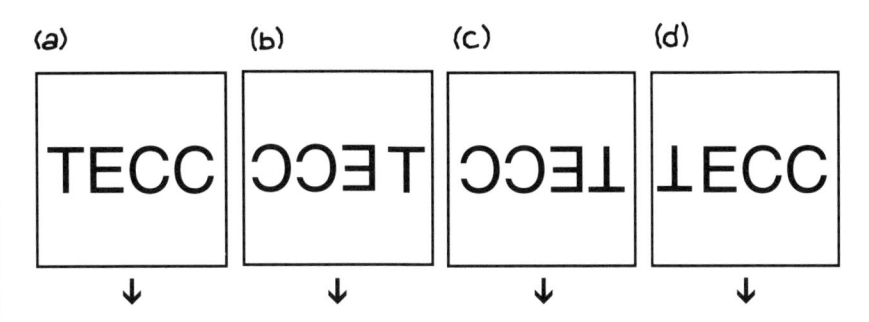

(a) TECC   (b) ⊃⊃ƎT   (c) ⊃⊃ƎT   (d) TECC

The slide will be put into the projector with the person using it facing the screen.

2. If you wanted the image on the screen to be larger, what would you do?

3. What type of lens is used to focus light from the slide on to the screen?

4. What is the job of the condenser lenses in the projector?

5. If the fan failed to work, what might happen to the slide?

Task 2

1. After you have read what Mr. Mearns said to Mr. Gelsthorpe, explain to one of your friends how a slide projector works. Make a copy of the diagram that Mr. Mearns drew. Write your own notes to help your explanation.

2. What would happen if a *concave* lens was fitted at the front of the projector instead of a *convex* lens?

3. How could you design the projector so that the problem mentioned in question 5 could not happen?

Light in Our Eyes

This activity should help you to understand how your eyes enable you to see.

David went to Mr. Lightman, the optician, to have his eyes tested. While he was there, he asked Mr. Lightman to explain to him how our eyes work.

First of all, Mr. Lightman showed him a diagram of a cross section of an eye.

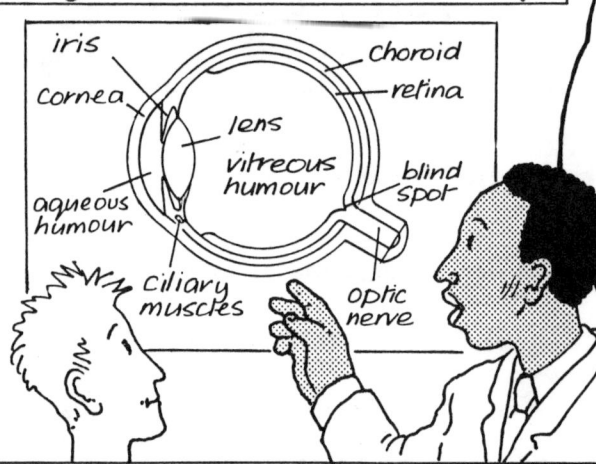

Each eye is like a small ball, about 2.5 cm in diameter, with a small, transparent bulge called the CORNEA at the front. Each eye fits into a socket in the skull and can be moved by muscles so that you can look in various directions without moving your head. Your eyelids move up and down over the cornea and spread liquid over it to keep it clean - rather like windscreen washers and wipers on a car. The CHOROID is a black layer which helps to cut out reflection inside the eye.

Your ability to see is provided by two kinds of light-sensitive cells in the RETINA, called RODS and CONES. The RODS are sensitive to the amount of light entering the eye and the CONES are sensitive to colour, but they only work well in strong light. The place at the back of the eyeball where the optic nerves leave is called the BLINDSPOT, because there are no cells there to pick up light.

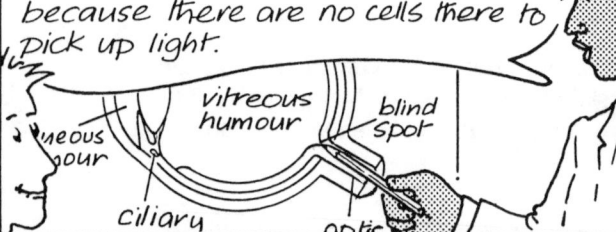

When light enters an eye, it is bent (refracted) mostly by the cornea and then by the LENS, which fine-focuses it onto the retina. The shape of the lens is changed by the CILIARY MUSCLES around it, depending on whether you are looking at a nearby object or at something a long way away. The ability of the lens to change its shape, and hence its focal length, is called ACCOMMODATION.

The coloured part at the front of your eye is a ring of muscle called the IRIS. At its centre, it has a hole called the PUPIL, which is just in front of the lens. The iris helps to control the amount of light entering the eye. In bright light, the iris expands and the pupil becomes smaller. If less light enters the eye the opposite happens.

If the intensity of light changes very suddenly, a chemical reaction also occurs, but this takes a few minutes. This is why your ability to see is impaired for a while when you go indoors on a bright sunny day.

When light from what you have been looking at is focused onto the retina, the image stays for about 0.1 sec. If you were in a room with no light at all and then a light was switched on and off about twenty times a second, you would think it was on all the time because one image would merge into the other. This is why when you visit the cinema or watch T.V., the picture looks as if it is continuously moving. Pictures are changing on the screen about twenty-four times every second.

© 1991 Folens Limited — This page may be photocopied for classroom use only

Why do we have two eyes?

Our two eyes give us an image of what we look at from slightly different positions. Our brain puts these two pictures together and we get a kind of 3D picture that makes the things we look at have depth. Things stand out like a 'pop-up' picture in a book. With one eye, we get a much 'flatter' picture of things. Our two eyes also help us to judge distances more accurately. Trying to put a jar onto a shelf in front of you is much more difficult, with one eye closed. You can't be sure when to let go of the jar.

The image formed on the retina of the eye is upside down, but our brain has learnt to turn this image the correct way up.

Thanks, Mr. Lightman, but one thing I don't quite understand. What is inside the spaces between the retina, lens and cornea?

When you have cut up a sheep or cow's eye, you will have noticed how hard it seems to be. This hardness is caused by the pressure of the two thick liquids in the eye.

The AQUEOUS HUMOUR and VITREOUS HUMOUR are like thin, clear colourless jellies. When you cut into the eyeball, the pressure is released as the jelly escapes and the eyeball collapses.

Thanks, Mr. Lightman. I think I can now answer the questions our science teacher set us.

Task

1. Explain how you can see what is going on in front of you in all directions without having to move your head.

2. Which part of your eyeball refracts light the most so that it focuses on to the retina?

3. Why is the inside of your eyeball black?

4. What is it inside your eyeball that controls the amount of light getting to the retina?

5. The retina has two types of light-sensitive cell. What are they and why can they only show us a picture in shades of grey at night?

6. What is the job of the lens? Explain clearly, with sketches, how the lens helps us to see objects far away and close to us.

7. How does the eye cope with very bright light and what problems are caused when we go from a bright, sunlit garden, to the inside of our house?

8. Why do we have two eyes?

9. How do T.V. pictures and cinema pictures fool our eyes into thinking we are looking at real movement?

10. Why does an eyeball feel so hard, as if it were solid?

11. Our eyes, like a camera, see images upside down. Draw a picture to explain why this is so.

Mirror, Mirror on the Wall

This activity will help you to understand about reflections.

Angela was telling Jodie about the video she had seen the night before.

'It was all about vampires! This man was a vampire, but nobody knew until he walked in front of a mirror.'

'What's so different about that? Did his reflection in the mirror look odd?' said Jodie.

'No, that's the point. There was no image in the mirror at all; that's how you can tell someone is a vampire.'

'That's daft, Angela. Mr. Foster told us in our science lessons that all things have an image in a mirror if there is any light.'

'Yes, I know, it was only a story. Anyway, I was away from school when you did those experiments on mirrors with Mr. Foster, so can you explain to me exactly what a mirror is and how it makes images?'

'Well I'll try, Angela, but I think you had better read the notes I wrote in the lessons first.'

Mirrors and how they work

Mirrors reflect light. Their smooth, shiny surfaces do not scatter light in all directions in the way that a rough surface does. A mirror reflects light in one or more directions. Any shiny, smooth surface can be a mirror. If you look at the surface of a pond when there are no ripples, you can see an image of yourself. Mirrors used by campers and those found in emergency survival kits are made of metal, such as polished stainless steel. Mirrors can be made by sandwiching a thin layer of aluminium between two layers of thin colourless plastic, which can be made in large sheets and cut to any shape or size. Glass mirrors are made by putting a smooth, very thin film of metal onto a sheet of glass. In most mirrors this metal is aluminium, but in mirrors where the best possible reflection is needed, silver is used. A special kind of paint covers the metal to stop it peeling off.

light hitting a rough surface

light hitting a smooth surface.

'I can understand all that but I still don't see why we see what we see', said Angela.

'Let's try an experiment, Angela, to see if I can explain it to you. You remember in '*Alice Through the Looking Glass*', Alice climbed inside the mirror. Well, your image in a flat mirror appears to be as far inside the mirror as you are in front of it. Because the light travels in straight lines, you appear to have turned round and faced yourself.'

message on screen

image of message in mirror

ANGELA IS LATERALLY INVERTED

Task

1. Explain how an ordinary sheet of glass can be made into a mirror.

2. Explain why you cannot see a reflection of yourself in all surfaces even if there is plenty of light.

3. What is written on the chalkboard behind Angela? What does it mean?

4. Write a message of your own on a piece of paper which can only be easily read by looking in a flat mirror.

5. Angela's image is the same size as her real self and she is 2.5m in front of the mirror. How far would Angela have to walk, if she could climb inside the mirror, to meet her own image?

6. Use pictures to explain why Angela appears to be brushing her hair with her left hand in the mirror, but is really brushing it with her right hand.

Keeping an Image

This activity will help you to learn how to use a camera more successfully.

When the native people of North America first saw photographs of themselves they were very frightened. They thought the camera had captured their spirit and that it was now trapped in the photograph!

We know this is not true, but photographs can be amazingly lifelike. Cameras have been used to record history for nearly 150 years. All cameras are really just light-proof boxes, the insides of which are matt black. This is so that light coming into the camera does not reflect off any surface inside but is all absorbed by the film to produce the photograph. The **lens** in a camera collects and bends the light so that it is focused on to the **film** at the back of the camera.

A camera with just a pinhole at the front and no lens at all can take a photograph if there is plenty of light available.

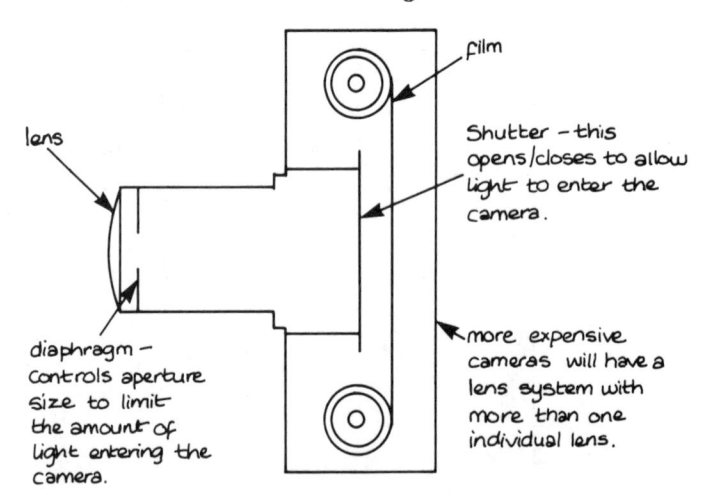

Diagram: cross-section of a camera showing:
- *lens*
- *diaphragm – controls aperture size to limit the amount of light entering the camera.*
- *film*
- *Shutter – this opens/closes to allow light to enter the camera.*
- *more expensive cameras will have a lens system with more than one individual lens.*

In more complicated cameras, lenses can be moved nearer or further away from the film to sharpen the focus of the image. Simple cameras are 'fixed' focus and are all right for taking photographs of friends or family on the beach, or anywhere where the distance from the camera to whatever is being photographed is 5-10m. The simpler, cheaper type of camera will not take close-up photographs where whatever is being photographed is closer than 1m. The lens cannot bend the light enough to focus it on to the film. Even very cheap cameras have some way of controlling the light entering them. The diaphragm in a camera is like the iris in your eye. The hole in the diaphragm in a camera is like the iris in your eye. The hole in the diaphragm is called the **aperture**. In some cameras, this aperture can be changed in size.

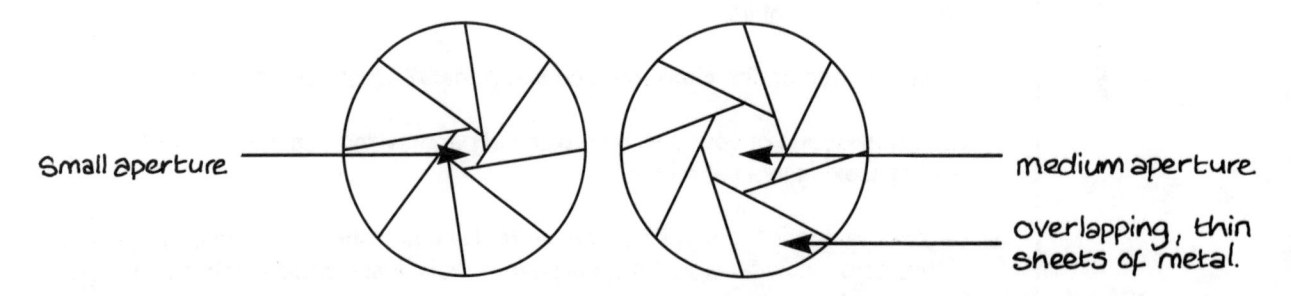

Diagram: two aperture illustrations labelled:
- *Small aperture*
- *medium aperture*
- *overlapping, thin sheets of metal.*

In the cheaper type of camera, there is a disc behind the lens with holes of different sizes in it, like that in a microscope you may have used. A ring around the edge of the camera can be turned to move a different hole into position. Symbols on the edge of the ring tell you which hole to use for the weather conditions. A large hole will let more light on to the film, a small hole less light. In more expensive cameras, the aperture is marked in **f-numbers**. An aperture of f 11 means that the diameter of the hole is 1/11 of the focal length of the lens.

© 1991 Folens Limited   This page may be photocopied for classroom use only   Page 14

The symbols used for the different sizes of aperture in cameras are shown below.

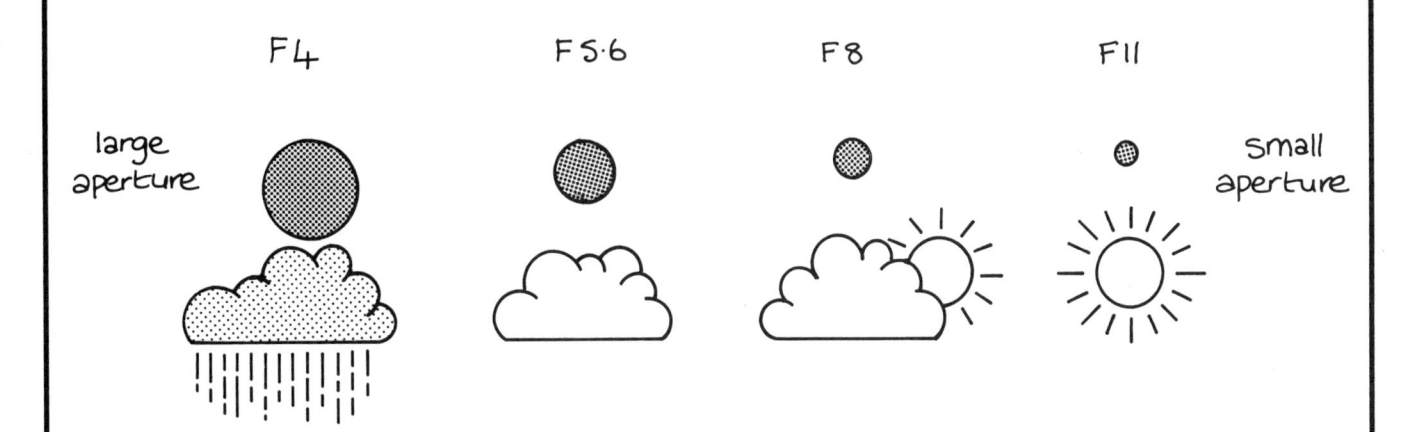

F4	F5.6	F8	F11
large aperture			small aperture

Cameras today come in a great range of sizes and shapes. There are Compact 35mm, SLRs, Disc cameras and Compact 110. The 35mm, 110 & 120 seen on a camera or film describe the width of the film itself.

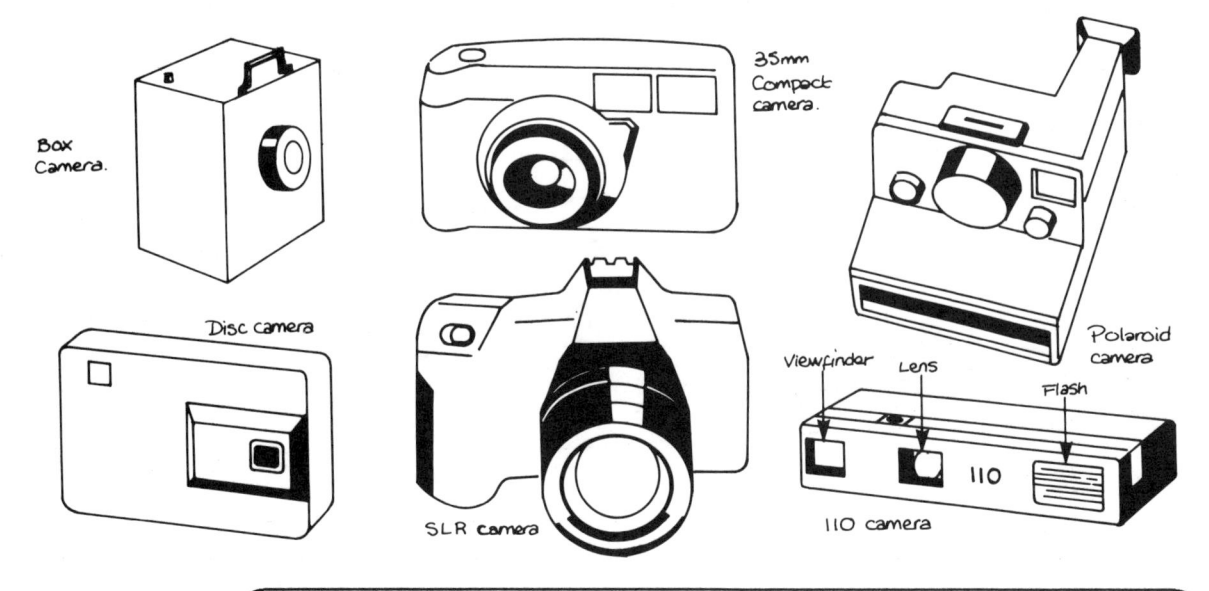

Box Camera.
35mm Compact camera.
Polaroid camera
Disc camera
SLR camera
Viewfinder Lens Flash
110 camera

Task

1. Why is the inside of a camera black?

2. What is the difference between 35mm and 110 film?

3. If you were taking a photograph of a family group in hazy sunshine, what aperture would you use? What would happen if a smaller f-number was used?

4. Cheaper cameras have a 'fixed focus'. What does this mean and why does it mean that these cameras cannot take photographs of objects closer than about 1m?

5. What size of aperture would you use if you were taking a photograph in dull, cloudy weather? Explain why you have chosen the aperture you have.

Eyesight Problems

This activity will help you to understand what effect wearing spectacles has on people's eyesight, and why some people need to wear them but others don't.

Sally has normal sight in each of her eyes. Light is reflected from whatever she is looking at and is focused sharply on to the retina of each of her eyes. Sally has no problem focusing light from distant objects or from objects that are as close to her as 15cm.

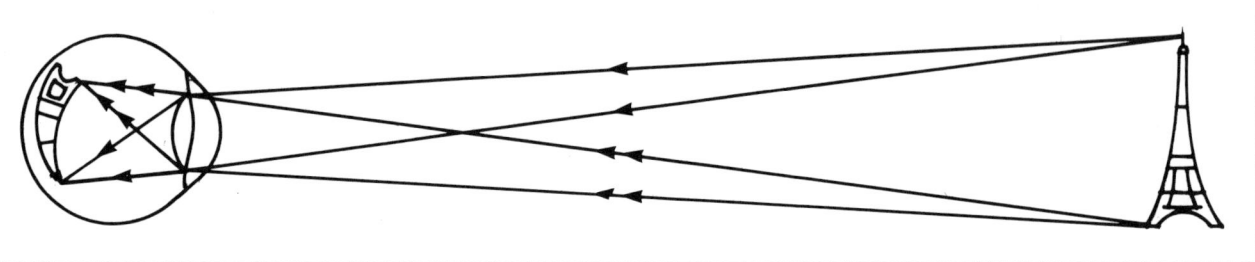

Zoe is **short-sighted** and cannot clearly see things that are a long way away. When she looks at the Eiffel Tower, the image of it on her retina is out of focus and is blurred. She can, however, see things that are close to her very clearly. Zoe's eyeballs are too long. To correct Zoe's short sight, the optician gives her spectacles with **concave** lenses.

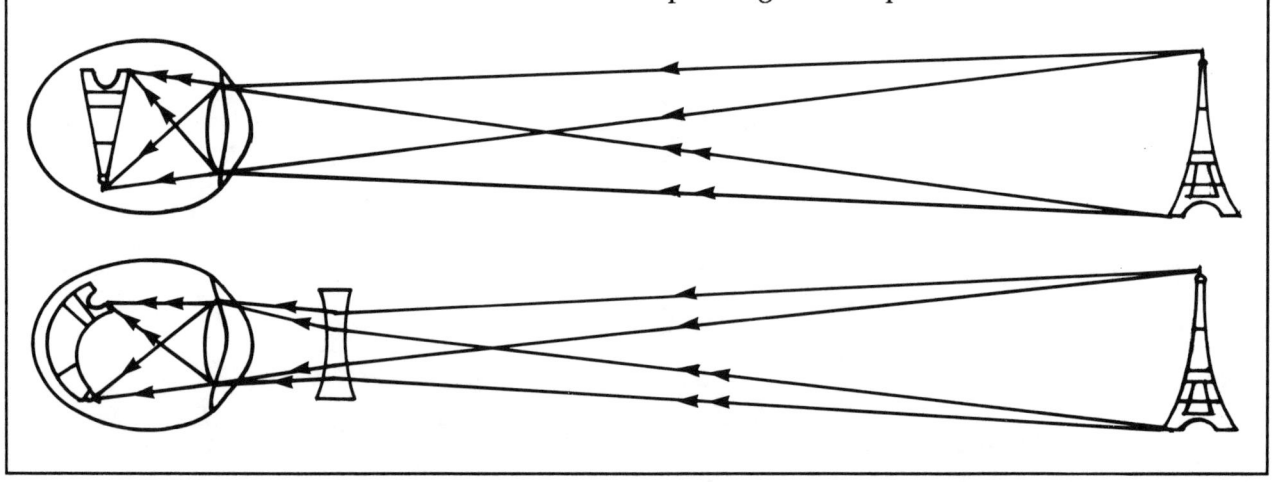

Mark is **long-sighted** and has the opposite problem to Zoe. He can see objects a long way away but cannot focus the words on the page of a book very easily. Mark has eyeballs that are too short and the retina is too close to the lens. Mark has to wear spectacles with **convex** lenses.

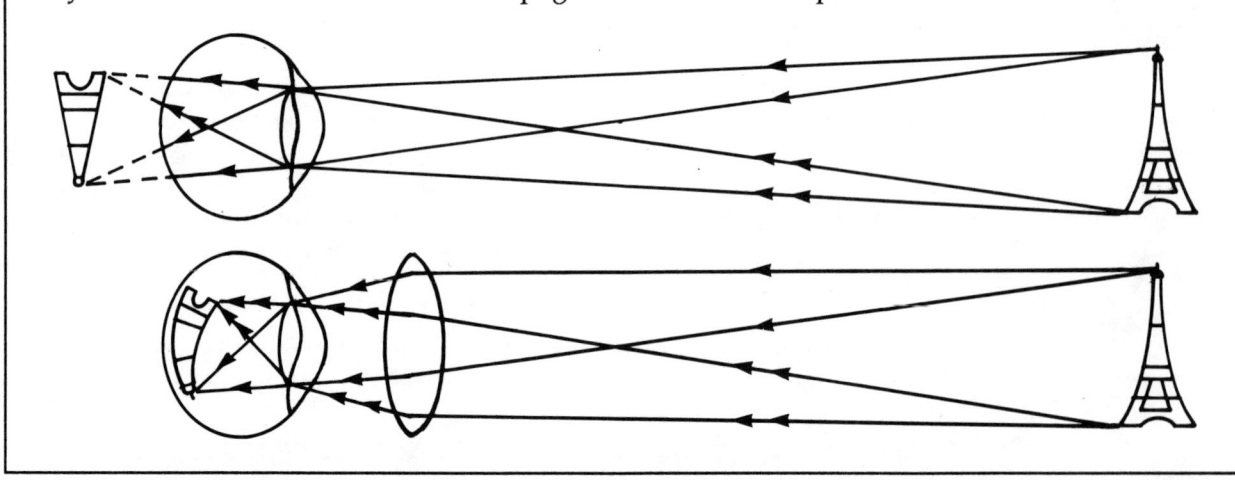

When you are young your eye lenses can easily change shape. This is called **accommodation**. The eye lens is made fatter so that we can see things that are close to us, and thinner for seeing things far away.

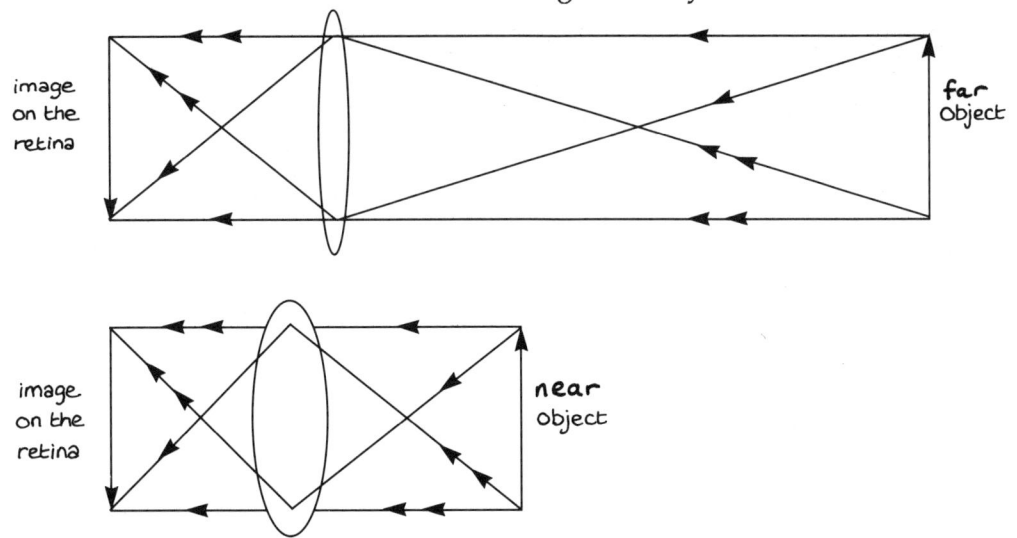

Sally's grandfather, John, has to wear spectacles for reading. His **long sight** has been caused by the lenses in his eyes becoming less flexible. This means that the lenses cannot bend the light enough to focus an image of the print in a book on to the retina of his eyes.

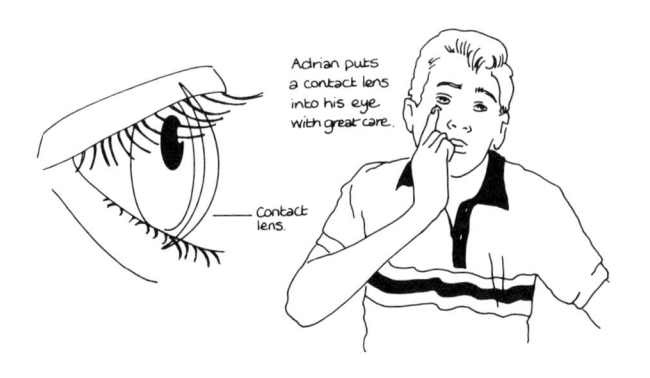

Adrian wears **contact lenses** instead of spectacles. When he turns his eyes, the lenses move as well. This means that he always looks through the lenses and not past the edges, as you do sometimes when wearing spectacles. Whatever you look at also looks more natural in size. When you look through spectacles, you look through different parts of the lens as your eye moves. If objects are looked at through the edge of a lens they can look distorted.

Task

1. If you have *short* sight, what is wrong with your eyes and how is it solved?

2. What type of lens is used to correct *long* sight?

3. What does *accommodation* mean?

4. What type of lens would Sally's grandfather have in his spectacles to help him to read the newspaper more easily?

5. What are contact lenses and why do they give a more natural picture of what is being looked at?

6. Find out why we have two eyes. (Hint - hold a pencil upright on the bench and very quickly try to touch the top of it with the tip of a finger. Now try the same experiment with one eye closed!)

© 1991 Folens Limited   This page may be photocopied for classroom use only

Light Law

This activity will help you to learn more about reflection and about different kinds of mirrors.

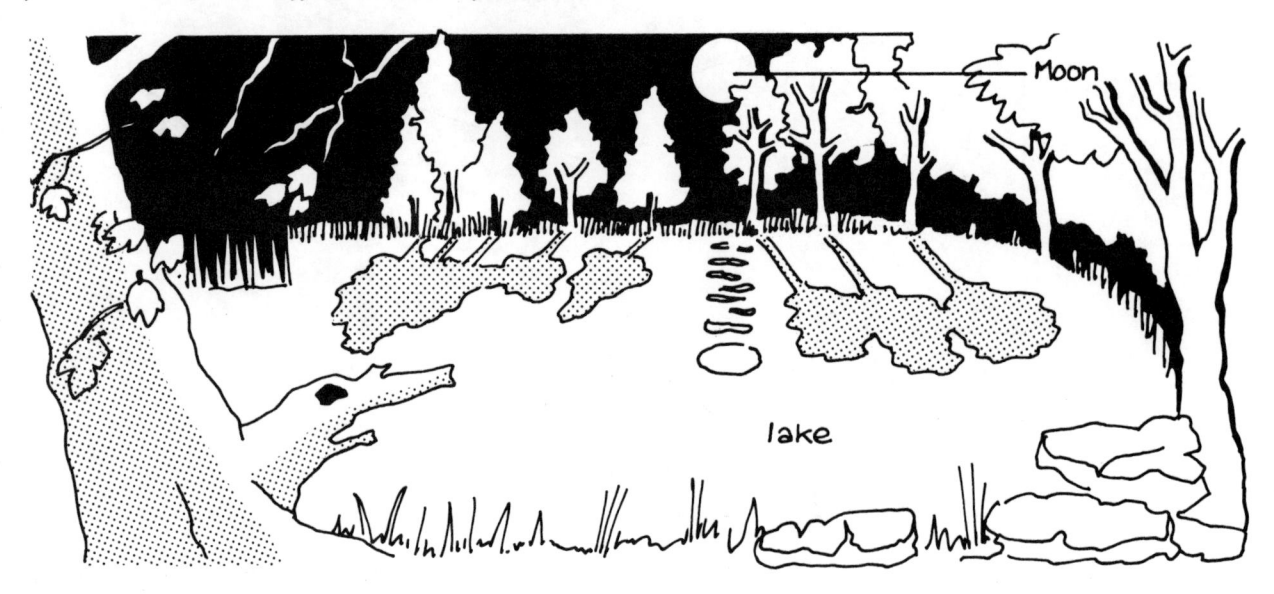

Jill and Leah were using an optics kit to investigate what happens to light when it hits a flat mirror. They have been told by their teacher that polished, smooth surfaces reflect light falling on to them in a regular pattern. Flat sheets of glass, calm water and polished sheets of metal are good **reflectors**, as well as mirrors. Flat surfaces that look fairly smooth, like this sheet of paper, reflect some light but not in any kind of regular pattern.

The diagram shows how the two girls set up their experiment.

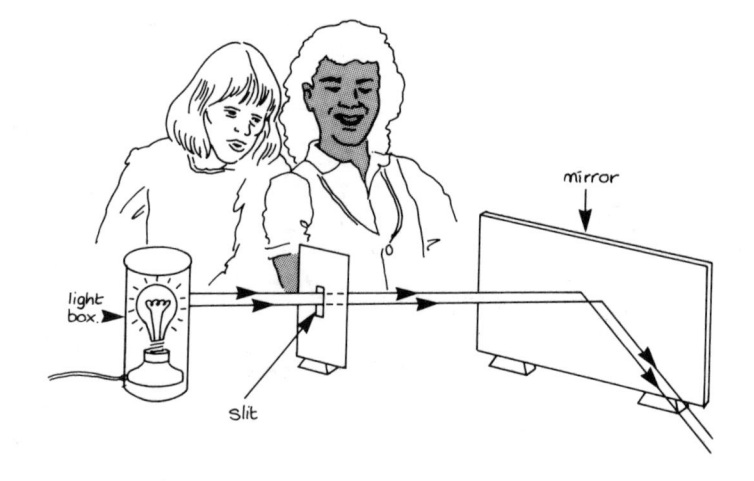

Here are the drawings of the light rays that Leah made in her notebook. All the angles are drawn actual size.

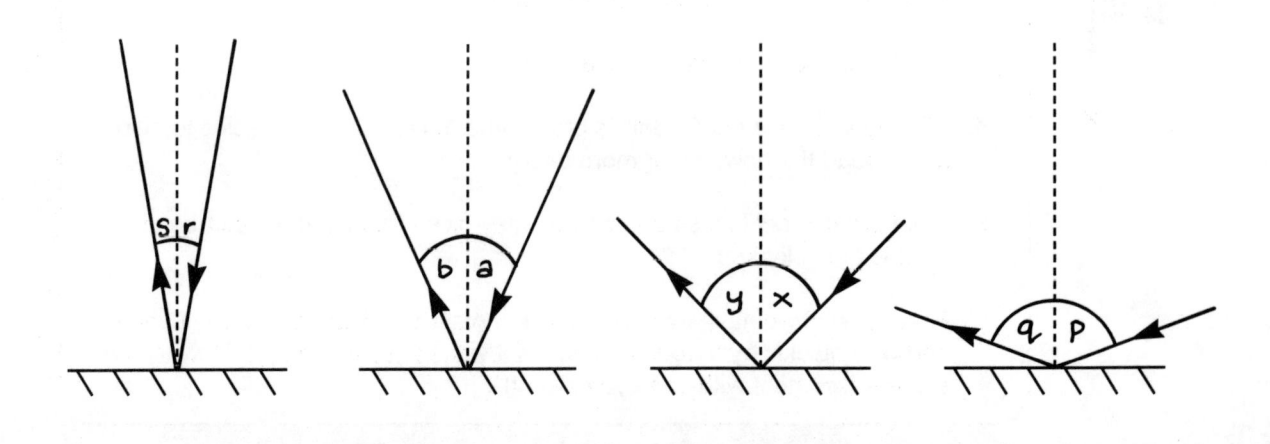

Angles *r*, *a*, *x* and *p* are called angles of **incidence** (*i*) and *s*, *b*, *y* and *q* are called angles of **reflection** (*r*). The ray of light hitting the mirror is the **incident** ray. The ray of light leaving the mirror is the **reflected** ray. Each dotted line in the diagram is called a **normal** and is drawn at 90° to the surface of the mirror.

Task 1

1. Draw up a table of data to show the angle of incidence and the angle of reflection for each part of the girls' experiment. The diagrams are drawn accurately, so you will need a protractor to measure the angles.

2. Can you infer any kind of pattern in the data? If so, what is it?

3. Redraw *one* of the girls' diagrams and fully label the angles, rays of light and the normal.

4. Make a drawing to show what would happen if Jill and Leah shone a ray of light along the line of the normal to hit the mirror at 90°. Write a sentence to explain what happens.

Task 2

Not all mirrors are flat. The two mirrors below are curved; one is a **convex** mirror the other is a **concave** mirror. Draw each of the mirrors and label which you think is convex and which concave. The concave mirror is used as a reflector for lamps. The convex mirror is found near the ceiling in the corner of shops. Why? Convex mirrors can also be seen at the top of the stairs in double decker buses. Why?

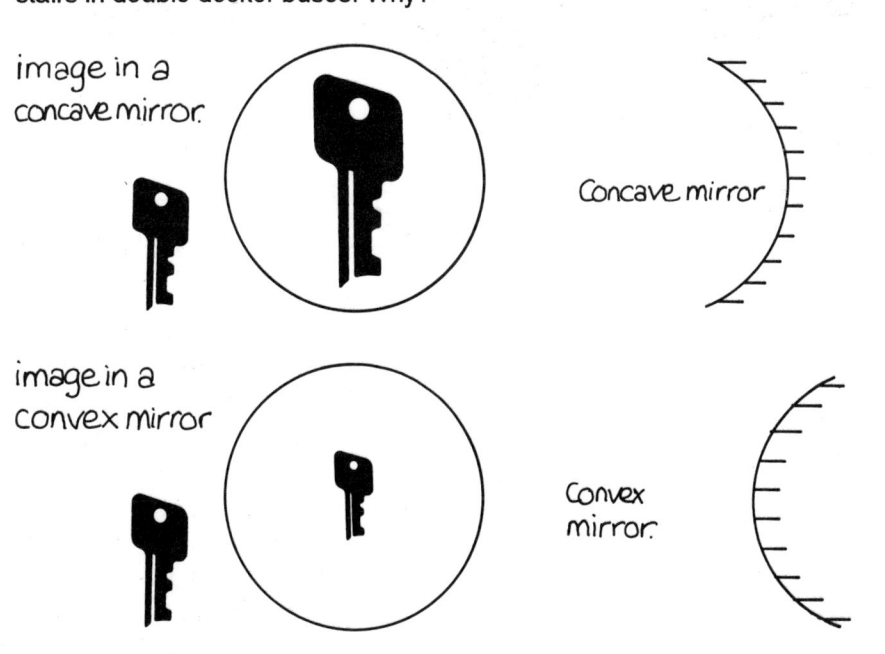

image in a concave mirror.

Concave mirror

image in a convex mirror

Convex mirror

© 1991 Folens Limited — This page may be photocopied for classroom use only

Back-to-Front Reflection

This activity will enable you to learn more about reflection and the meaning of lateral inversion.

It is April 1st and Sandra and Abdul decide to play a joke on their English teacher. Abdul writes the following message on the chalkboard:

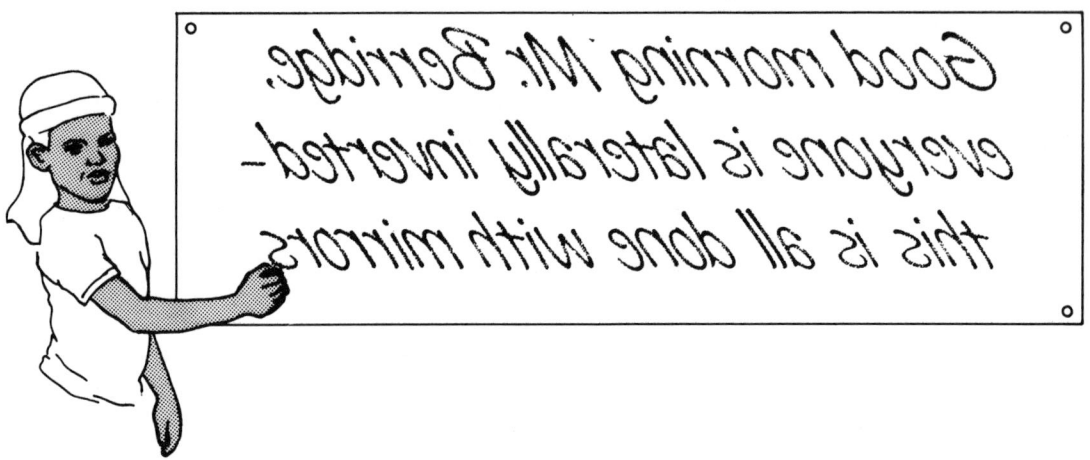

Good morning Mr. Berridge, everyone is laterally inverted - this is all done with mirrors.

The picture we see in a mirror is called the **image** but it is not completely the same as the real thing (the **object**). If you scratch your right ear, your image scratches its left ear! Everything in the image is turned sideways and we say that the image is **laterally inverted**. The sign on the front of an ambulance is often back to front as may be the name of a company on its lorries.

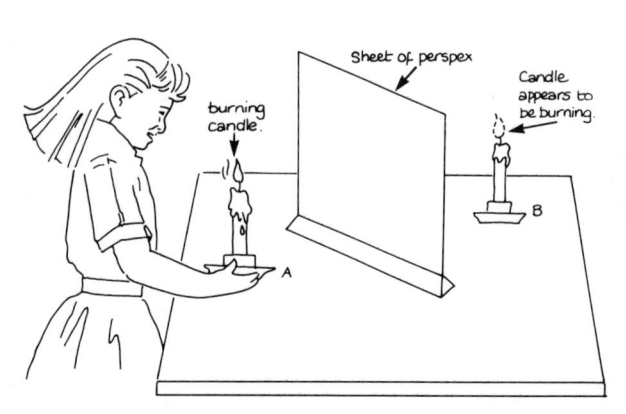

When you stand in front of a **plane** (flat) mirror, your image is still the same shape and size as you normally are. Your image also appears to be just as far into the mirror as you are in front of it.

Sandra carried out an experiment to see if she could get any evidence for this idea. She collected two bench mats and placed a candle on each. Between the bench mats she stood a sheet of clear perspex. Only the candle nearest to her, Candle **A**, was lit.

Sandra looked through the perspex so that she could see the reflection of the lit candle. She then moved the candle nearest her so that the other one also looked lit, with the flame of the first candle appearing to sit on the wick of the unlit one. She measured the distance of each candle from the sheet of perspex before moving candle **B** and repeating the experiment.

Sandra's data

Distance of candle A from the perspex	Distance of candle B from the perspex
10cm	10cm
12cm	12cm
15cm	15cm
18cm	18cm
20cm	20cm
23cm	23cm

Task

1. What is written on the English teacher's chalkboard and how could it be easily read?

2. Why do ambulances and some lorries have their names written back to front?

3. Write your own name so that it can only be easily read by looking in a mirror.

4. What can Sandra infer from the data she collected in her experiment?

5. In the story *'Alice through the looking glass'*, Alice climbs inside the mirror to meet herself. If Alice stood three metres in front of the mirror and the Madhatter was two metres behind her, how far away from the Madhatter would Alice's image be?

All Done with Mirrors

This activity will help you to learn about some of the practical uses of mirrors.

If you watch a game of snooker, at some time in the game one of the players will need to bounce the cue ball off a cushion to reach the ball they want to 'pot'. Light bounces (**reflects**) off a flat mirror in the same kind of way.

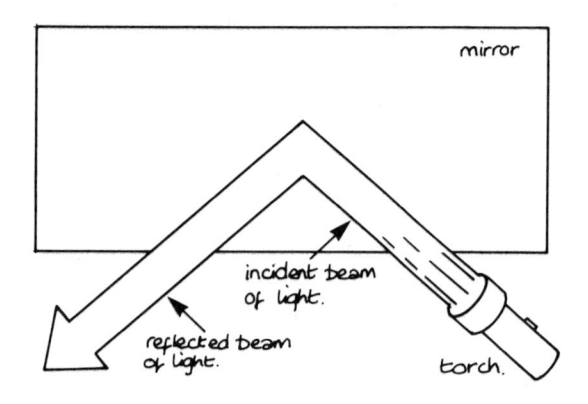

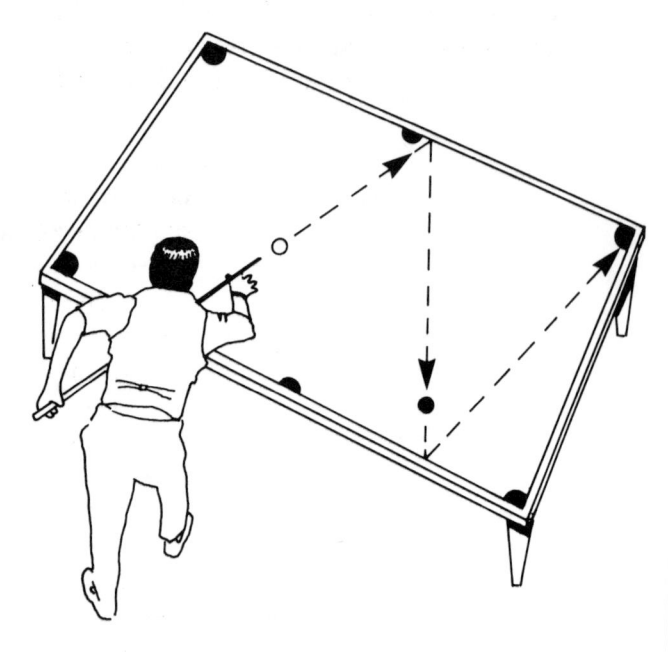

The light from the torch beam reflects off the surface of the flat mirror at the same angle that it hits it. This is what scientists call the **first law of reflection**.

Mirrors have many uses apart from being useful to check that your hair is tidy!

Curved mirrors can magnify objects or they can make things look smaller. A **concave** make-up mirror curves inwards and magnifies part of a person's face so that she can put make-up on more easily. A **convex** mirror bulges outwards and makes things look smaller but it lets you see more of what is going on around you. A security mirror in a shop is convex. It lets the store detective get a good view of what is going on around a shop.

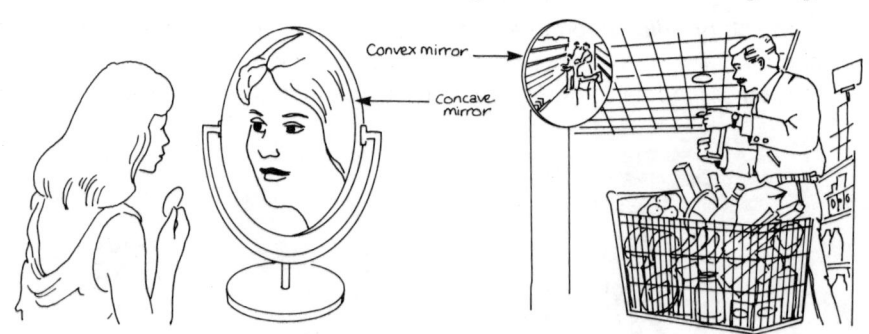

Even flat mirrors can be used to look around corners. If the opening to a field or the drive of a house is near the corner of a road, a mirror can be placed nearby so that drivers of cars, lorries or tractors leaving the field or drive can see that the road is clear.

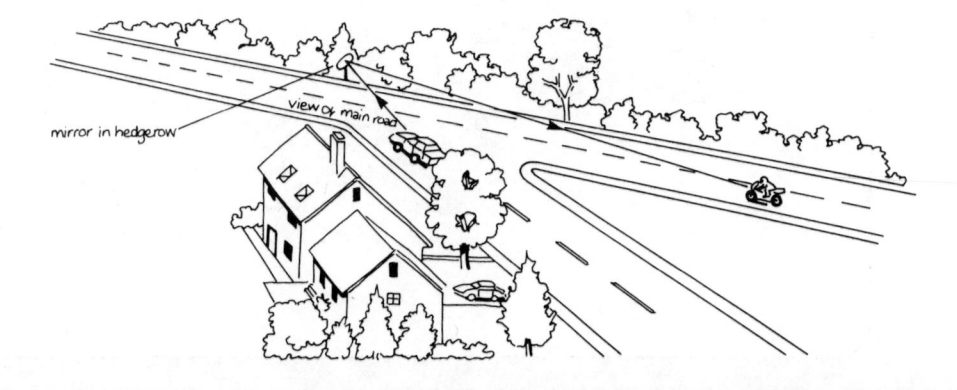

Periscopes use the idea of reflection to look over or around things. Submarines have periscopes to allow them to see above the surface of the water when the submarine itself is below the surface. Whenever there is a big public occasion, very simple periscopes are used by people at the back of the crowd to get a good view of what is going on.

The diagram on the right shows a simple periscope made with two flat mirrors fixed at 45° to the frame of the periscope.

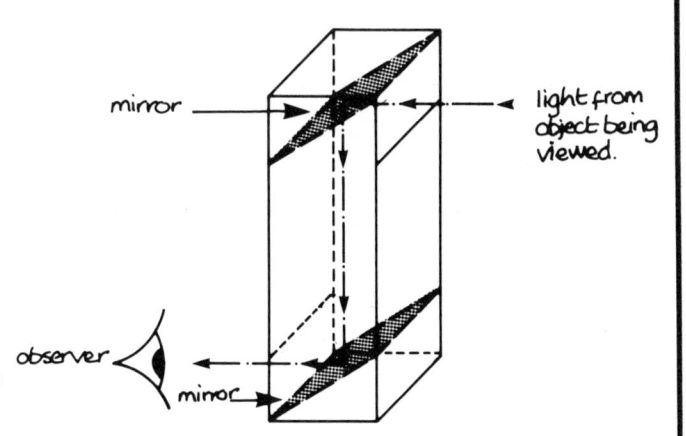

Task

1. Make a list of all the mirrors that you can think of in different places and write down what they are used for. Try to find out if they are flat, concave or convex mirrors.

2. Try to explain in your own words, with the help of a picture, what the first law of reflection is.

3. Use the plan on the right to make your own periscope. You need to draw the outline of the periscope on thin card. Cut along the **solid** lines and score and bend the card along the **dotted** lines.

   Card mirrors covered with a thin sheet of aluminium can be glued into place or plastic mirrors can be used. The mirrors need to be 7cm by 5cm rectangles.

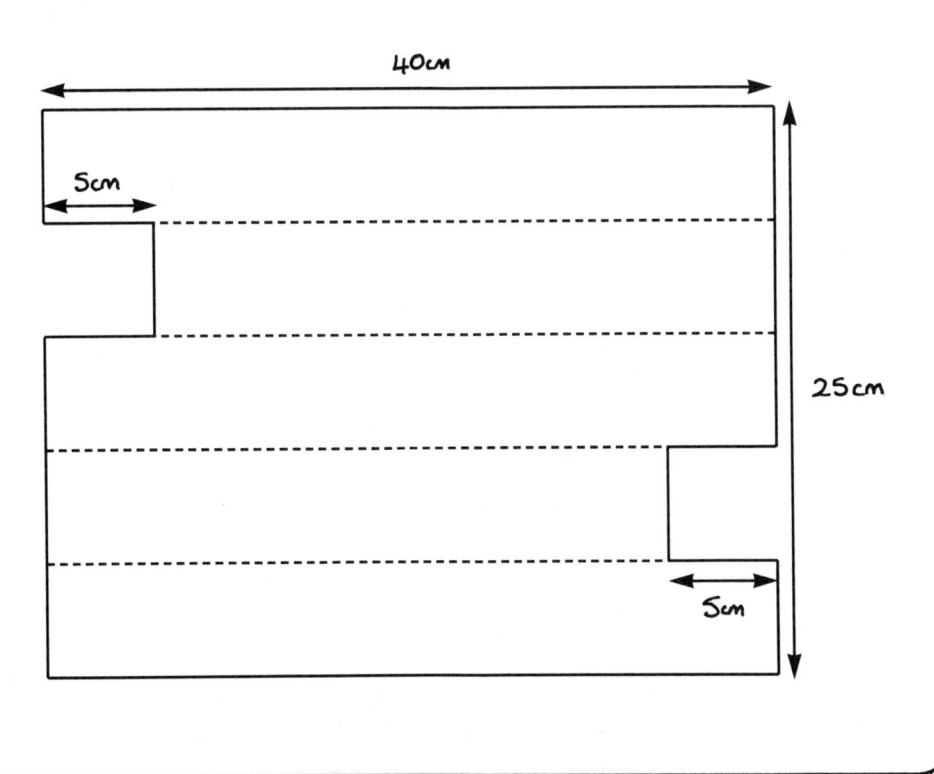

© 1991 Folens Limited   This page may be photocopied for classroom use only   Page 23

Moving Pictures

This activity will help you to understand how movement is produced in a film.

Note to teachers: Pupils will need copies of 'flick book' pictures on page 26 for Task 1.

Chetan and Lee were going to the cinema to see their favourite new space adventure.

As they sat in the cinema, Lee said that he could not understand how everything looked so real when he knew that he was looking at a flat screen. Chetan offered to explain to him how the people and the spacecraft were made to look alive and moving.

1) The film is thrown onto the screen by a projector. A powerful beam of light is passed through the transparent film and the picture is magnified by lenses so that we see a large image of the film on the screen. The film is really made up of thousands of small pictures called frames. The film is loaded into the projector on what's called the feed spool and after passing through the projector it's collected by the take-up spool.

Diagram labels: Film 'feed' spool, Film, Shutter, Mirror, light, lenses, claw, Focusing lens, Gate, 'Take-up' spool

2) The film is pulled through the projector by small metal claws which hook into the sprocket holes on each side of the film. A wheel with small metal teeth feeds the film into the 'gate' and another wheel guides it out on to the take-up spool. A shutter — which looks a little bit like a propeller — spins round in front of the film to interrupt the beam of light. Twenty-four separate pictures are passed through the gate every second. The shutter interrupts the light beam 48 times a second. The film really passes through the projector in a series of jumps. Everything happens so quickly that, even though a series of still pictures is projected on to the screen, you think you are seeing continuous movement. The film shutter and claws are moved by an electric motor today, but in the days of....

...silent movies a handle was turned on the side of the camera and projector.
The series of still pictures appears as a single moving picture because of something called 'persistence of vision'. When you look at an object light reflects from it on to the retina in your eye. If someone removes the object it takes the eye 0.1 s to realise that what you were looking at is no longer there! If the object you look at is very bright, you can still see an image for some time after this. So, when your eye sees 24 pictures every second, they overlap on the retina and you think you see movement. Each single picture is slightly different from the one before because they are taken with a camera which takes 24 pictures every second.

© 1991 Folens Limited — This page may be photocopied for classroom use only — Page 24

Task 1

Make yourself a moving picture flick book using the sheet given to you. Cut out the pictures from the separate sheet of paper. Punch a hole in the top left-hand corner of each picture and fasten them together with a paper fastener. Then flick them between your thumb and first finger of your right hand. Try to draw a flick book of your own!

Task 2

1. How many different pictures are projected on to the screen each second during a film?

2. Explain in your own words what 'persistence of vision' means.

3. What is the job of the shutter in the projector?

4. Why are there holes in the edge of a piece of film?

5. Colour in and cut out the two pictures shown below. Stick each picture on to a piece of card. To the back of one of the pieces of card, tape a thin piece of wooden dowel or a pencil. Glue or tape the two pieces of card back to back. Roll the piece of dowel or pencil between the palms of your hand.
What do you see and why?

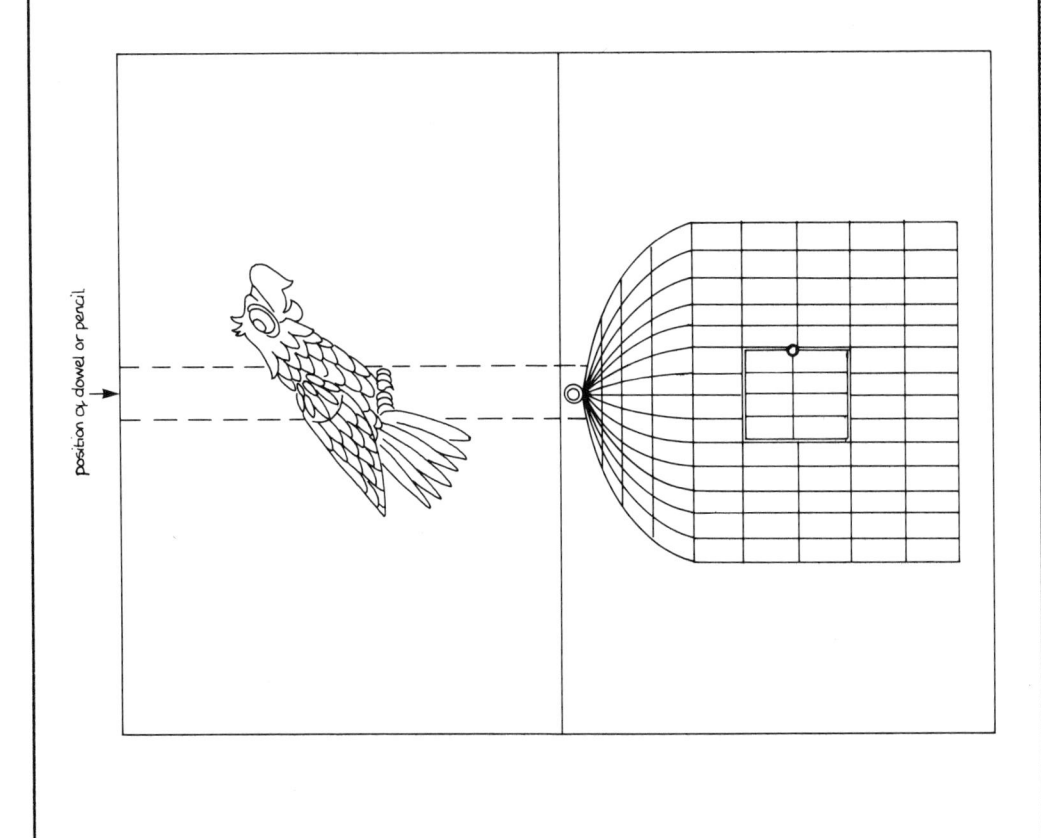

© 1991 Folens Limited   This page may be photocopied for classroom use only   Page 25

© 1991 Folens Limited   This page may be photocopied for classroom use only   Page 26

Electromagnetic Spectrum

Wavelength (metres)		
10^4	long wave	
		Radio
10^2	medium wave	
	short wave	
$10^0 (=1)$	VHF	T.V.
10^{-2}	UHF	Radar
	microwaves	Microwave oven
10^{-4}		
	infra red	Electric fire
10^{-6}		
10^{-8}	visible light	
	ultraviolet	People sunbathing
10^{-10}	x-rays	X-ray for hospital use
	gamma rays	Nuclear power station
10^{-12}		

© 1991 Folens Limited — This page may be photocopied for classroom use only

Waves All Around

This activity will teach you about electromagnetic waves.

Note to teachers: Pupils will need copies of 'The Electromagnetic Spectrum' on page 27 for Task 2.

Chetan and Andrew have been given a piece of homework. They have to find out what the **'Electromagnetic Spectrum'** is.

Below are some of their notes, made from books they looked at, together with a diagram their teacher gave them.

Chetan's notes

○ A man called James Maxwell came up with the idea in 1864 that light waves were really electric and magnetic fields vibrating. A German man named Heinrich Hertz made radio waves travel across his laboratory with an electric spark. He did this in 1887.

Scientists today think that light and radio waves are part of the same spectrum.

The waves are like invisible water waves.

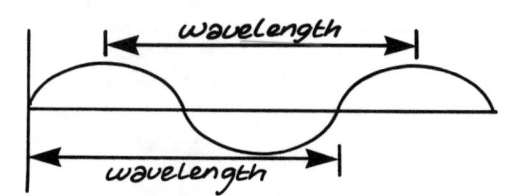

○ Waves are made by electrons vibrating. These vibrations are called the frequency of the wave. 'High frequency' means 'lots of vibrations each second.' The frequency of the vibrations is named after Mr. Hertz.

Andrew's notes

○ Electromagnetic waves can move through space at 3×10^8 m/s. At this speed, it only takes 8 minutes for light to reach us from the Sun. These waves are different from sound waves. Sound waves need something to travel through, but electromagnetic waves don't. If a wave has a high frequency, its wavelength is small.

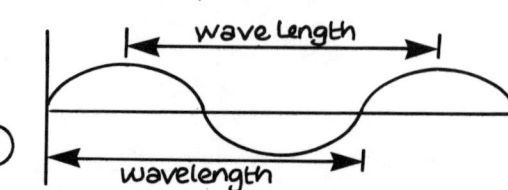

○ Different colours of light have different wavelengths. Red light has the longest wavelength.

Task 1

1. What type of wave has the shortest wavelength?

2. Which colour of light has the shortest wavelength?

3. What does ultra-violet light do to us?

4. What are X-rays used for?

5. What type of waves are given out by electric fires?

6. What did James Maxwell think caused light waves?

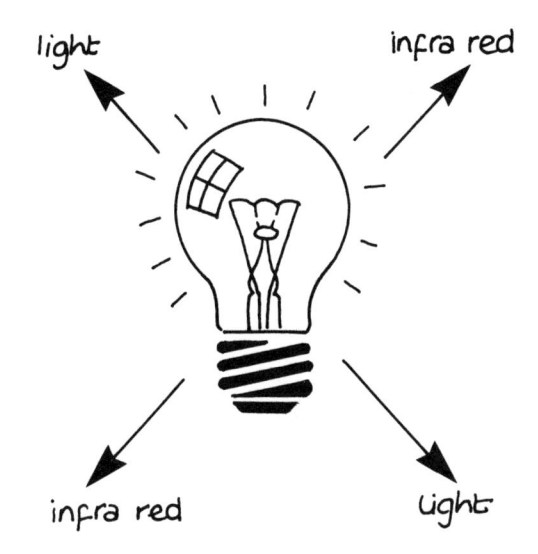

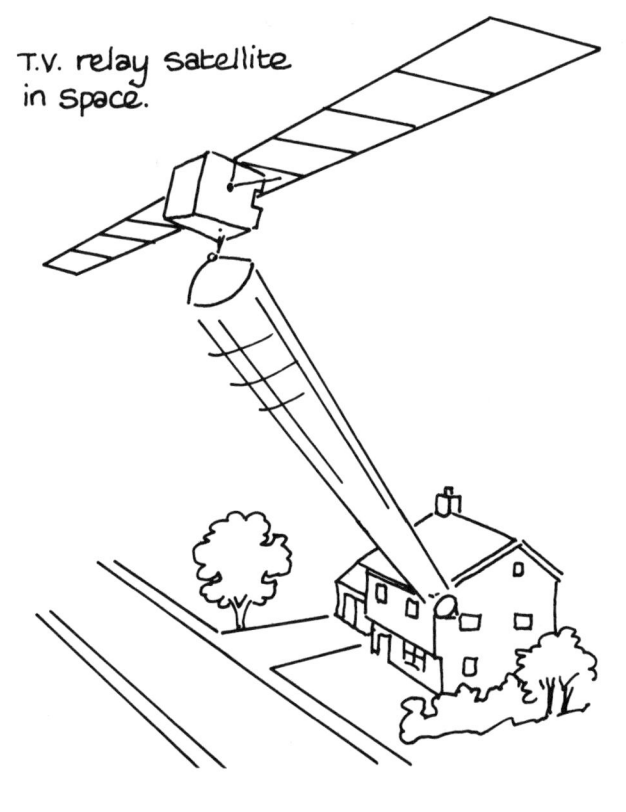

Task 2

1. Who sent a radio wave from one end of his laboratory to the other?

2. What disease is treated with Gamma rays?

3. What do UHF and VHF mean and where would you find them being used?

4. How long does it take light to travel to us from the sun?

5. Draw your own version of the electromagnetic spectrum. Add pictures to show how we use the different types of waves.

Hear Ear!

This activity will help you to understand how your ear works.

Rebecca   Petra

Petra was late arriving at school one day. Mrs Friedman, her science teacher, knew why but her friend Rebecca did not.

'Where have you been, Petra?' 'Oh, I've been to the doctor to have my ear syringed because it was blocked up with wax. I can hear really well now.'

Rebecca asked Petra if she knew how her ears worked and why having wax in them stopped you hearing so well.

'Well I wasn't sure, so while I was at the doctor's I asked him to explain what goes on when we hear a sound.'

> Your ears collect vibrations that we call sound, and change them into electrical signals that the brain can make sense of. When anything vibrates it makes a sound, but we can only hear these vibrations if they are between 20 and 20,000 vibrations a second. A dog, however can hear vibrations (frequencies) above 20,000, which is why we can't hear a dog-whistle. Pigeons can hear a sound caused by something that takes 10 seconds to produce one vibration! A pigeon can hear sounds with frequencies from 0.1 to 20,000 vibrations a second. A moth can pick up frequencies of nearly 1 million vibrations a second!

> We can hear sounds even when the vibrations travel through a solid. We can almost feel the sound. Sound can also be heard under water. Whale noises can be heard by other whales hundreds of kilometres away. Blue whales can produce sounds as loud as a jet aircraft! We normally hear sound vibrations that travel through the air. When sound vibrations reach us they are collected by the PINNA – the outer ear. This behaves like a funnel letting the vibrating air pass down the EAR CANAL to hit your EARDRUM, a thin sheet of skin stretched across the end of the ear canal. The vibrating air makes the eardrum vibrate.

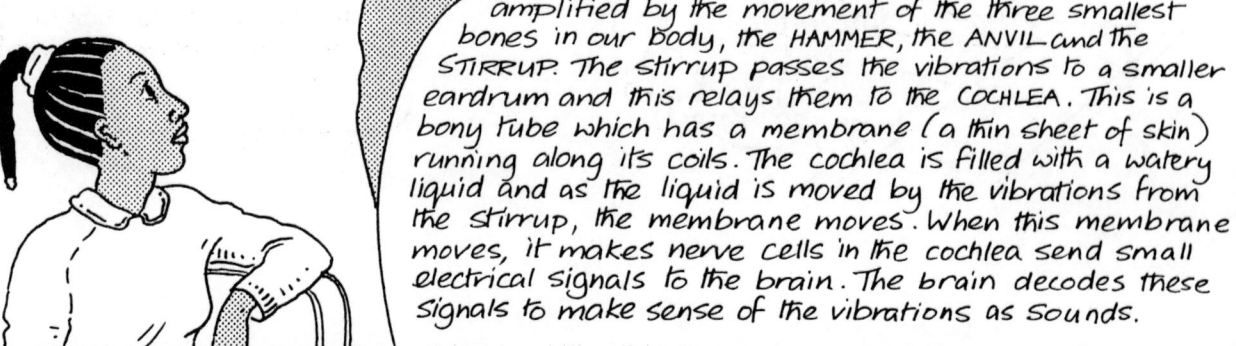

Diagram labels: semi-circular canals, anvil, hammer, nerve to brain, ear canal, cochlea, hairs, stirrup, pinna, ear drum, Eustachian tube, (Outer ear filled with air), (Middle ear filled with air), Inner ear (filled with liquid)

> The small vibrations of the eardrum are amplified by the movement of the three smallest bones in our body, the HAMMER, the ANVIL and the STIRRUP. The stirrup passes the vibrations to a smaller eardrum and this relays them to the COCHLEA. This is a bony tube which has a membrane (a thin sheet of skin) running along its coils. The cochlea is filled with a watery liquid and as the liquid is moved by the vibrations from the stirrup, the membrane moves. When this membrane moves, it makes nerve cells in the cochlea send small electrical signals to the brain. The brain decodes these signals to make sense of the vibrations as sounds.

© 1991 Folens Limited — This page may be photocopied for classroom use only

The semi-circular canals in our ears are like spirit levels. They control our balance.

For you to hear properly, nothing must get in the way to stop vibrating air moving down the ear canal. Wax can block the canal, and if it hardens it is difficult for any sound to make the eardrum vibrate.

For your ears to work correctly, the air pressure on each side of the eardrum needs to be equal. If the EUSTACHIAN TUBE, leading to the back of the throat, becomes blocked, air pressure builds up in the MIDDLE EAR and you find it difficult to hear. If you have a cold, the Eustachian tube can become blocked with catarrh.

Ring ring! Ring ring! Ring ring!

"Can't you hear that phone!"

The air pressure inside an aircraft changes as the aircraft climbs. This change in the cabin air pressure can cause pain in the middle ear and affect your hearing. Eating a sweet or holding your nose and swallowing hard can help to make the air pressure in your middle ear the same as that in the aircraft cabin.

Task 1

1. What normally vibrates to carry sounds to our ears?

2. What range of frequencies can we hear if our ears work well?

3. Why can't we hear a dog-whistle?

4. What is the purpose of the three small bones in the middle ear?

5. Explain in your own words how our brain 'hears' sound. Draw a diagram of an ear to help you.

6. What is the purpose of the Eustachian tube? What happens if it becomes blocked?

7. What was an ear trumpet? What was it used for?

8. Why can pigeons and moths hear things that we cannot?

9. Give an example to show how well sound can travel through water.

Sound Survey

This activity is about the loudness of sound, how it is measured and the levels which can endanger hearing.

The loudness of sound can be measured in units called **decibels**. Claire and Jody carried out a sound survey of their school and the village in which they lived. Their science teacher had given each pair of pupils a **decibel meter** to measure the sound levels.

The girls collected the data in the following table:

Type of Sound	Loudness measure in decibels (dB)
people talking normally	50
two people whispering	30
the school library	20
traffic outside the school	80
jet aircraft flying overhead	130
road drill outside the school	120
a door slamming	75
caretaker using a vacuum cleaner	70
telephone ringing	65
disco music in the youth club	110
lathe in the workshops	85
typewriter in the school office	60

1. Redraw Claire and Jody's table, arranging the data so that the loudest noise is at the top and the quietest one is at the bottom.

2. Use the girls' data to draw a graph, with **loudness in dB** up the side of the graph and the **types of sound** along the bottom.

The girls knew that loud sounds could damage their ears, but they did not know how loud the sounds had to be to do this. They decided to go to the school library to see what else they could find out about the loudness of sound and how it was measured. The notes that they copied from the books they looked at are shown below:

"The loudness of sound is measured in decibels (dB)."

"0dB does not mean no sound. It is the lowest sound level that humans can hear. It is called the **threshold** of hearing."

"Sounds become uncomfortable to us if they are above 120dB".

"Sounds above 140dB cause pain and damage to our ears."

"Sudden loud noises above 140dB can rupture (tear) our eardrums."

"We live in a noisy world where sound can be a kind of pollution and make life unpleasant and even dangerous."

"Drivers of tractors, operators of machines in factories and people who use pneumatic drills should wear ear protection."

"Cotton wool plugs in the ears can cut down noise by 10dB. Plastic ear plugs can cut down noise by 30dB. Ear defenders can cut down the noise level by 50dB."

Task 2

1. Could any of the sounds that the girls recorded permanently damage your hearing?

2. Which sounds in the girls' data table could you infer were sound pollution? What evidence do you have to be able to make your inferences?

3. Use the information that the girls collected to write your own notes called 'Sound can damage your ears'.

4. Design a safety poster to alert people in a noisy factory to the danger to their hearing. Your poster should encourage them to wear ear plugs or ear defenders.

Noise or Music?

This activity should help you to understand how sounds are produced and the difference between a noise and music.

Note to teachers: Pupils will need copies of page 36 in order to complete Task 2.

Sound, like heat and light energy, travels through the air in waves. Sound waves are **longitudinal waves**. The air particles vibrate from side to side and so bunch together and then spread out. This causes changes in pressure in the air. The largest distance which the particles move from their starting point is called the **amplitude** of the wave.

A **tuning fork** is designed to vibrate at a certain frequency, but you may find it difficult to see it vibrating. If, however, the vibrating tuning fork is held next to a ping pong ball suspended from a piece of thread taped to it, you can see the ball bounce backwards and forwards.

Compression (a region of higher air pressure.)

Rarefaction (a region of lower air pressure.)

• = particles of air moved by a vibrating tuning fork.

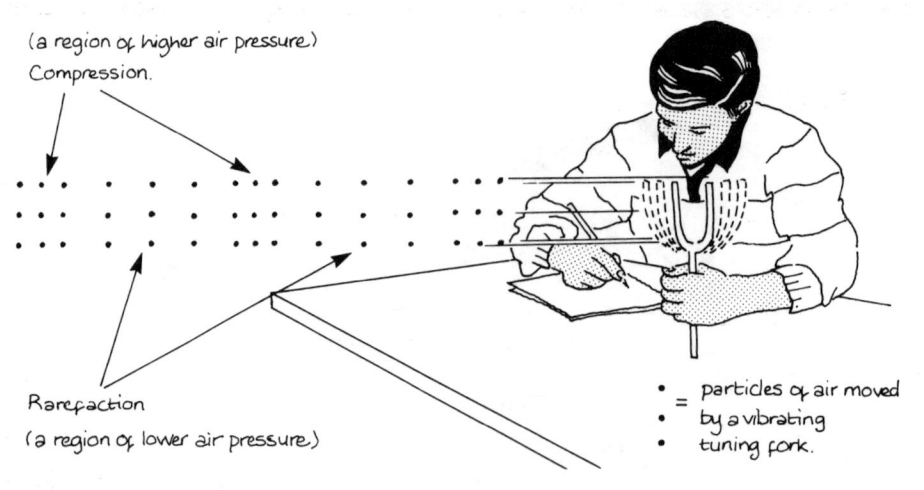

If the tuning fork vibrates and you hear the sound, you can infer that something between the fork and your ear must be vibrating.

The distance between corresponding points on consecutive compressions or rarefactions is called the **wavelength** of the wave.

The number of times a particle moves backwards and forwards in a second is called the **frequency of a wave**, measured in **hertz (Hz)**. Humans can hear sounds with frequencies between 20Hz and 20,000Hz.

Most sounds are a mixture of frequencies. As you walk along a street, the sound you hear is 'noise'. It has no pattern because the frequencies are not connected.

If the frequencies are in **harmonics** (multiples of one frequency), connected to one basic frequency, we hear notes. This combination of sounds is what we call music. Some combinations of frequencies seem like music to one person and 'noise' to another!

© 1991 Folens Limited   This page may be photocopied for classroom use only

When a trumpet and a violin play the same note, they produce a vibration of the same frequency. This is called a **fundamental** frequency. The two instruments sound different because of the harmonics on top of this fundamental frequency.

The table on the right shows that different musical instruments have overlapping frequency ranges.

Instrument	Frequency Range
Trumpet	150 → 1000Hz
Violin	190 → 2700Hz
Flute	260 → 2050Hz
Piano	30 → 4100Hz
Double bass	40 → 250Hz

In a harp, there are strings of different lengths and thicknesses to produce different notes when the strings are plucked. A long, thin string can give the same note as a shorter, thicker one, but the long thin one has a better **tone**. A violin only has four strings of different thickness but the same length. However, the violinist can alter the length of each string by pressing her fingers down on the strings.

Task 1

1. Explain the difference between noise and music.

2. What range of frequencies can a person with 'normal' hearing pick up?

3. Design a chart or graph to compare the frequency ranges of the different musical instruments shown above. Your chart or graph needs to show how their frequency ranges overlap.

4. How can a person playing a double bass play more than four notes if the instrument only has four strings?

Task 2

On a separate sheet that will be given to you are pictures of some musical instruments. Complete the table with the name of the instrument and also say what vibrates to produce the sound.

Instrument	Name	What vibrates?
A		
B		
C		
D		
E		
F		
G		
H		
I		
J		
K		
L		

© 1991 Folens Limited — This page may be photocopied for classroom use only

Speed of Sound

This gives you one example of how the speed of sound through air can be measured.

Eleanor and Helen carried out an investigation to try to measure the speed of sound.

The girls went outside the school to the wall of the gymnasium and measured a distance of 50m from it. They took with them a stop clock and two flat pieces of wood to bang together. They chose the wall of the gymnasium because any sound made in front of it gave a good echo. Helen started banging the two pieces of wood together so that she could hear BANG! - echo - BANG! - echo - in a regular pattern. When she had built up a rhythm, Eleanor timed how long 20 BANGS! took. She counted the first BANG! as zero. The girls tried the experiment six times.

Working out the speed of sound:

The sound travelled 100m between a BANG! and its echo. That meant that between the first two BANGS! the sound had travelled 200m. In the time it took for 20 BANGS! the sound travelled 20 x 200m = 4000m.

The girls then found the speed of sound by dividing the average time for 20 BANGS! into the distance the sound travelled in that time, or

$$\text{Speed of sound (m/s)} = \frac{\text{distance travelled by sound}}{\text{average time for 20 BANGS!}}$$

Eleanor and Helen's data table:

Attempt	Time for 20 BANGS! (seconds)
1	12
2	13.5
3	12.5
4	13
5	14
6	11.5

Task

1. Why didn't the girls just time how long it took for the sound to reach the wall and bounce back once?

2. What is the average time taken for 20 BANGS!?

3. According to the girls' data, what is the speed of sound? Show your calculation as well as your answer.

4. Apart from the measurements that the girls made, what other variable could they have measured which affects the speed of sound?

History of Space Flight

This activity will help you to appreciate the progress made in space travel during three decades.

Year	Date	Craft	Event
1957	October 4th	Sputnik 1	launched by the Soviet Union. Orbited the Earth every 96min.
1960	November	Sputnik II	Laika, a dog, sent into space.
1961	April 12th	Vostok 1	A Russian, Major Yuri Gagarin, becomes the first man in space.
1961	May 5th	Liberty Bell 7	Alan Shepard, an American, is the first American in space.
1962	February 20th	Friendship 7	John Glenn - first American to orbit the Earth.
1962	August 11th ---------15th	Vostok 3 Vostok 4	Andrian Nikolayev Pavel Popovich
1963	June 16th	Vostok 6	Valentina Tereshkova - the first woman in space.
1965	March 18th	Voskhod	Alexei Leonov takes the first walk in space.
1965	June 3rd	Gemini 4	Edward White is the first American to walk in space.
1968	December 21st -------------- 27th	Apollo 8	James Lovell, William Anders, Frank Borman - first flight around the Moon.
1969	January 16th		Yeugeny Khrunov & Alexei Yeliseyev take part in the first spacewalk from Soyuz 5 to Soyuz 4.
1969	July 21st	Apollo 11	Neil Armstrong is the first man on the Moon, followed by Buzz Aldrin. Michael Collins stayed in the command module orbiting the Moon.
1969	November 14th --------------- 24th	Apollo 12	lands on the Moon.
1970	April 11th --------17th	Apollo 13	An explosion on the spacecraft on the way to the Moon forces the mission to be abandoned.
1971	January 31st - Feb 9th	Apollo 14	lands on the Moon.
1971	April 19th	Salyut 1	Soviet Union launches first space station. Manned for 23 days June 6th - 30th. All 3 men on board killed on the return flight in Soyuz 11.
1971	July 26th - Aug 7th	Apollo 15	lands on the Moon - an electric car used for the first time - travelled 17 miles.

1972	April 16th ------ 27th	Apollo 16	lands on the Moon.
1972	December 7th --------------19th	Apollo 17	- last Apollo mission.
1973	May 15th	Skylab launched	- the first American space station.
1975	July 16th ------ 18th		American Apollo 18 links up in space with the Soviet Soyuz 19 spacecraft.
1981	April 12th --------14th		First flight of the Space Shuttle 'Columbia'.
1983	June 18th		First American woman in space - Sally Ride in the Space Shuttle 'Challenger'.
1986	January 28th		Space Shuttle 'Challenger' explodes killing the crew of seven.

Task 1

1. Who or what was the first living thing to go into space?
2. When did the first man go into space and who was he?
3. When did the first woman travel through space and who was she?
4. What did the crew of Apollo 8 do?
5. What was the Russian Alexei Leonov the first person to do?
6. Neil Armstrong was the first person to land on the Moon. Who was the second?

Task 2

1. What did Michael Collins do on Apollo 11?
2. Why was Apollo 13 unlucky?
3. When was the last Apollo mission?
4. What unusual event took place in 1975 between July 16th and 18th?
5. When did the first car travel on the Moon and why did it not cause pollution?
6. What was the name of the American space station?
7. What happened on April 12th 1981?
8. Why was the Space Shuttle programme stopped for a while at the start of 1986?

© 1991 Folens Limited   This page may be photocopied for classroom use only

Moon Matters

This activity will help you to understand why the Moon looks different to us on Earth at different times of each month.

Chetan had been given a telescope for his birthday and was busy setting it up one evening when his friend, Neil, arrived.

'What are you going to look at, Chetan?', asked Neil.

'Ms. Pearce, our science teacher, has asked us to make observations of the Moon this month so that we can see how its **phases** change.'

During the month, the two boys drew pictures of what they saw through the telescope. They carefully recorded what they saw.

Neil also asked his father for some information about the Moon and was given the following printout from a database.

```
The Moon is 400,000 km away from the Earth and it has a diameter of 3500 km.
It takes the Moon 27.25 days to orbit the Earth once.
When we talk about moonlight we are talking about light from the Sun that is reflected off
the surface of the Moon. The Moon itself does not glow.
As the Moon moves around the Earth, its gravitational pull causes water to be dragged along
- this is what we call the tides. The Moon's gravity pull is only 1/6 of that of the Earth.
The Moon has no atmosphere and there is no water there. The Moon's surface is covered
in craters. When meteorites hit the Moon, they are not burnt up by an atmosphere.
The surface temperature of the Moon varies from 100°C to -155°C.
```

Task 1

Chetan's drawings of the phases of the Moon are shown below (a - h). Unfortunately, each drawing was on a separate piece of paper. Chetan dropped them and so the pictures are jumbled up. Trace, copy or cut out each of the pictures and stick them next to their correct position on the diagram showing the phases of the Moon (1 - 8).

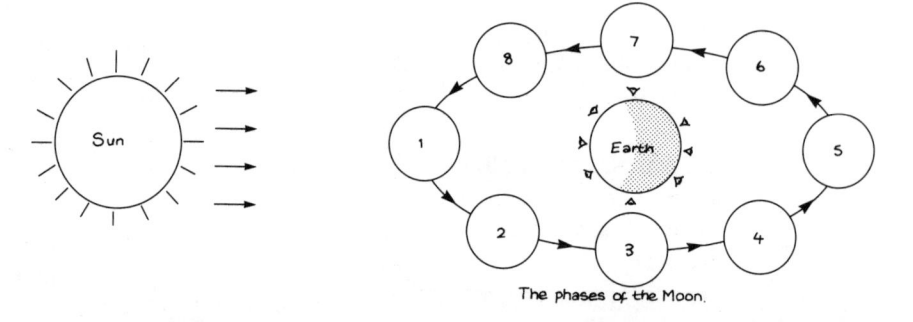

(a) (b) (c) (d) (e) (f) (g) (h) no moon visible

The phases of the Moon.

© 1991 Folens Limited — This page may be photocopied for classroom use only

The Moon was first visited by man on July 21st 1969 when Neil Armstrong and Buzz Aldrin landed from Apollo 11. The third member of the crew, Michael Collins, stayed in orbit around the Moon, in the command module, and did not land.

When you look at the Moon through a telescope, dark areas can be seen. Early astronomers called these areas **seas** because they thought they had water in them. Some of the craters on the Moon are very big; Copernicus is 90km in diameter, and some are more than 240km in diameter.

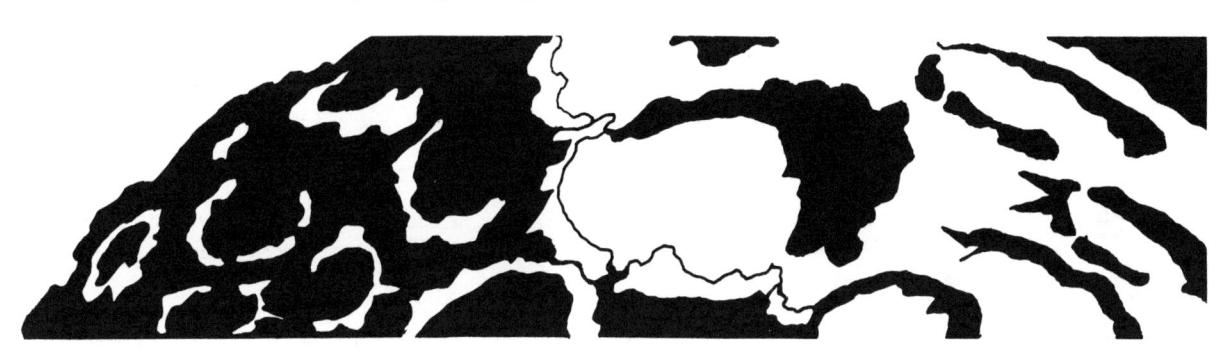

Task 2

1. Who were the first people to land on the Moon and when did they land?
2. Why did the astronauts on the Moon need a special suit with an oxygen supply?
3. Where was Michael Collins when the other two astronauts were walking on the Moon?
4. What would make it possible for Neil Armstrong to break the high jump record?
5. Why could you not swim in the seas on the Moon?
6. What is the temperature variation of the Moon's surface? Why is it so large?
7. Why are there so many craters on the surface of the Moon?
8. How long does it take the Moon to orbit the Earth once?
9. How far away from us is the Moon?
10. What connection is there between tides and the Moon?

Twinkle, Twinkle Little Star

This activity will teach you about the stars you see in the sky.

Amina was walking home with her friend Sophie. It had got dark early and it was already getting cold. 'I think it's going to be very frosty tonight, Amina' said Sophie. 'Yes, I think you're right Sophie. Look how clear the sky is; you can see lots of stars.' 'What are stars, Amina? Are they like planets?'

'I'm not sure, Sophie,' said Amina. 'My brother, Nazim, says you can see the planet Venus glowing in the sky at night, so perhaps they are like planets.' 'I think we ought to try and find out,' said Sophie. 'Reena told me that she had been doing a topic on the planets and that sort of thing in her science lessons at school. I bet we will be doing it soon.' 'O.K., Sophie. Let's go to the school library at lunchtime tomorrow and see what we can find out,' said Amina.

The two girls looked in several books and at a database in their school library. Sophie thought it would be a good idea to use the rough notes they had made and the printout from the database to make some notes that could be used in their science lesson.

'Why don't we type out our information on one of the word processors in the library,' said Amina.

Task

Printed below are rough notes that the two girls wrote down. Use these sentences to help you to write a page of work which explains what **stars**, **galaxies** and **constellations** are.

'A star is a bit like a human being! It is born, it grows up, it gets old and it dies.'

'Stars start life as a cloud of gas and dust called a **nebula**.'

'The gas and dust are pulled into a giant ball by the pull of gravity.'

'As the ball of gas and dust is pulled closer together it gets very hot and starts shrinking.'

'Nuclear reactions in a star give out lots of heat and light.'

`'Stars use hydrogen as their fuel.'`

'Stars swell and heat up when they have used up all their hydrogen, then they shrink to form White Dwarves.'

'Big stars suddenly explode at the end of their life to form **Supernovae**. These can be as bright as 100 million Suns.'

'Our Sun has been alive for about 5000 million years and is about half way through its life.'

© 1991 Folens Limited — This page may be photocopied for classroom use only

'When our Sun dies, it will form a Red Giant and will be big enough to swallow up the Earth, Mars, Venus and Mercury before it becomes a White Dwarf.'

'There may be as many as 100,000 million stars in a **galaxy**.'

'Nearly all galaxies have a regular shape, like a spiral or an ellipse.'

Spiral Galaxy

Elliptical Galaxy

'Our sun is in a spiral galaxy called the Milky Way.'

'Astronomers think the Universe may have as many as 10,000 galaxies in it.'

'The patterns that stars make in the night sky are called constellations.'

'There are over 80 constellations.'

'Names were given to the constellations by astronomers hundreds of years ago.'

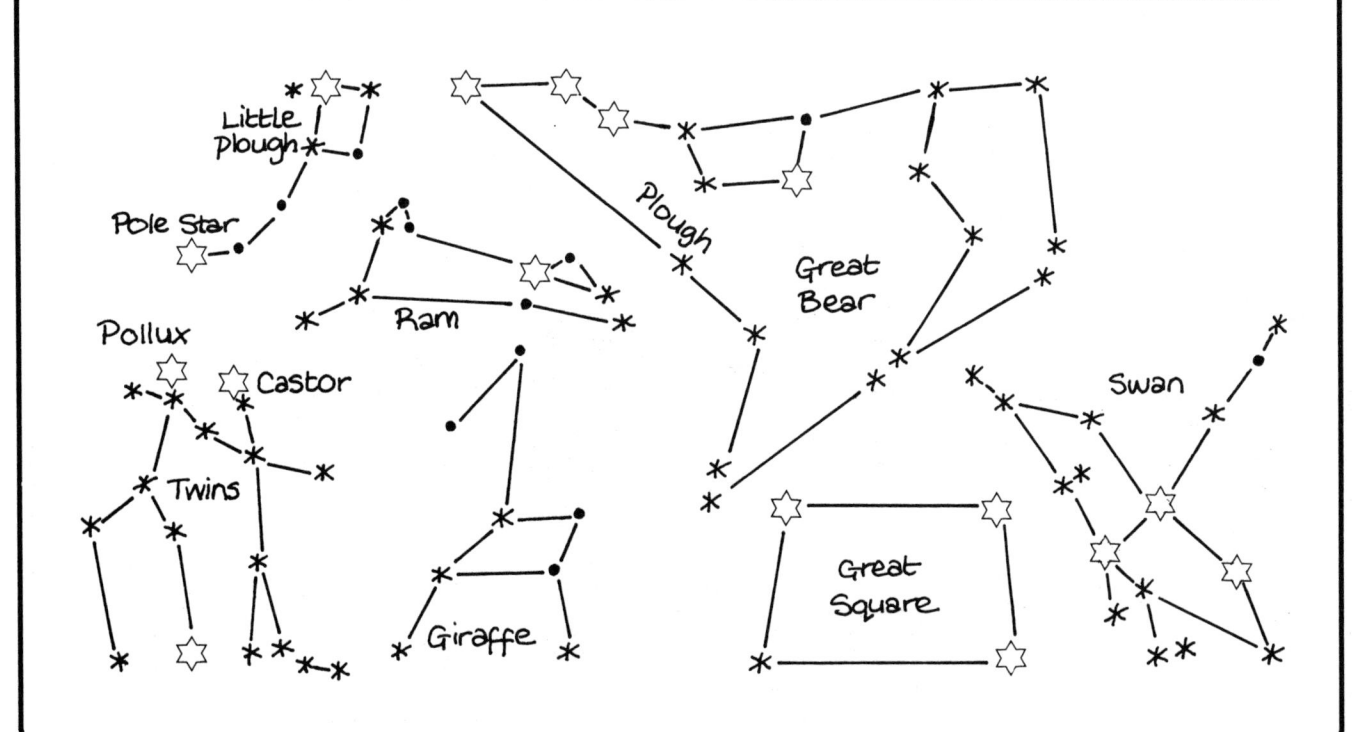

Little Plough
Pole Star
Pollux
Castor
Twins
Ram
Plough
Great Bear
Giraffe
Great Square
Swan

© 1991 Folens Limited   This page may be photocopied for classroom use only   Page 43

Seeing Stars!

This activity will teach you about the Sun and other stars.

My mum says that some of those stars are not there anymore!

Do you mean I'm imagining some of what I see?

No, I think my mum means that some of the stars are so far away that they have gone out and the light is still on its way to us.

Hold on, what do you mean - gone out?

Well, to be honest, Lee, I'm not quite sure. Let's ask Mr. Foster.

The two boys went to see their science teacher Mr. Foster.

Sir, what is a star?

...and how can they go out?

Well lads, our Sun is a star - a very small one compared with some others. Our Sun, like other stars, is a huge ball of gas. In the centre of the Sun, it is very hot. A continuous nuclear reaction gives out an enormous amount of energy. This energy is sent out into space as radiant energy. All the different types of radiant energy make up what scientists call the ELECTROMAGNETIC SPECTRUM. Our own sun has a surface temperature of approximately 6000°C, but the centre is over 20,000,000°C.

Lee looked rather worried.

If it's burning that hot, won't it run out of fuel and 'go out' soon?

Don't worry, Lee, astronomers think that there is enough hydrogen fuel left for well over 5,000,000 years! Some stars are very bright. One called Deneb is 60,000 times brighter than the Sun. It does not look that bright because it is 1400 light years away!

© 1991 Folens Limited — This page may be photocopied for classroom use only — Page 44

Panel 1:

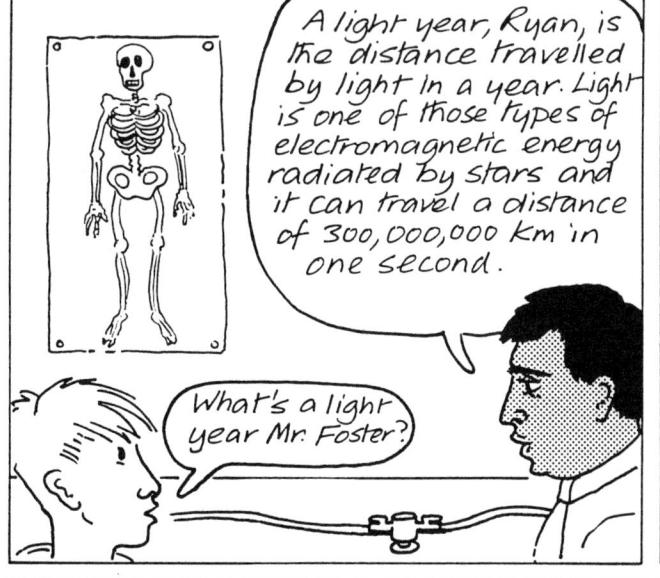

"What's a light year Mr. Foster?"

"A light year, Ryan, is the distance travelled by light in a year. Light is one of those types of electromagnetic energy radiated by stars and it can travel a distance of 300,000,000 km in one second."

Panel 2:

Ryan got out his calculator and tried to work out how many kilometres light could travel in a year. He soon gave up, the number was too big to fit onto the calculator display.

"You'll need a calculator that can show 16 digits on the screen! The nearest star to us apart from the Sun is Proxima Centauri, and that is 4.3 light years away."

Panel 3:

"What kind of gas are stars made of?"

- a cloud of gas in space.
- Star gets smaller due to the pull of gravity.
- Star begins to glow as it heats up.
- Star expands as a RED GIANT as it uses up its hydrogen fuel.
- Star becomes WHITE DWARF and explodes.

Astronomers think that all stars begin life as a cloud of hydrogen. As time goes on, gravitational forces cause the hydrogen atoms to be attracted to one another, and so the cloud shrinks. As the cloud shrinks the gravitational forces get stronger and the hydrogen fuses (sticks together) to make atoms of helium gas. As this change takes place a tremendous amount of energy is released. This process is called NUCLEAR FUSION. Here on Earth, scientists have discovered how to split atoms to release energy. This is called NUCLEAR FISSION, but they cannot yet do what the stars can do. When a star runs out of fuel it may explode or just shrink. Some stars are so far away that light is still on its way to us even though it 'went out' millions of years ago.

Task

1. How many kilometres away is the nearest star to our Sun? What is its name?

2. Explain why the star Deneb does not appear brighter than it is, compared with our Sun.

3. Why does Lee not need to worry about the Sun 'going out' soon?

4. What is meant by nuclear fusion?

5. What do astronomers believe all stars began life as, and what happens to them to make them shine so brightly?

6. Find out what 'Red Giants' and 'White Dwarves' are.

7. On a piece of paper - without a calculator - find out how many kilometres light can travel in a year.

8. Why are some of the stars that Lee looked at no longer there?

© 1991 Folens Limited — This page may be photocopied for classroom use only

Our Solar System

This data handling activity will teach you about the planets in our solar system.

Look carefully at the data table, then complete the tasks.

Planet	Diameter (km)	Distance from the sun (km)	Surface temp (°C)	Atmosphere (main parts)	Number of moons
Earth	12,750	1.5×10^8	-88 to +58	oxygen nitrogen	1
Jupiter	142,800	7.8×10^8	-25	hydrogen ammonia	at least 16
Mars	6,790	2.3×10^8	-125 to +30	carbon dioxide	2
Mercury	4,880	5.8×10^7	-180 to +420	none	none
Neptune	48,600	4.5×10^9	-160	methane	2
Pluto	3,300	5.9×10^9	-220	?	1
Saturn	120,000	1.4×10^9	-110	hydrogen ammonia	at least 20
Uranus	52,300	2.9×10^9	-160	methane	at least 15
Venus	12,100	1.1×10^8	+475	carbon dioxide nitrogen	none

Task 1

1. Which is the nearest planet to the Sun?
2. Which planet has the largest diameter?
3. How many moons does Jupiter have?
4. Which planets have an atmosphere like that of Earth?
5. On which planet does the surface temperature vary the most?
6. Name the planet which is the nearest to Earth.
7. Which is the coldest planet? Think of one reason why it is so cold.
8. Name the smallest planet.
9. Find out which planets have 'rings'. What do astronomers think these rings are?

Task 2

Join together two pieces of A4 cm graph paper. Join the bottom edge of one to the top edge of the other. Lay the sheets out horizontally. You are going to make a scale drawing of the planets in the solar system. Imagine the Sun is on the left. Draw circles to represent the planets. Use a scale of 1cm to 14,000km. Draw the planets in the correct order, moving out from the Sun. Do not try to draw the distances between the planets to scale - just space them out equally.

Teachers' Notes

GENERAL NOTE

No direct practical work is set in any of the pieces of work in this book, but should a teacher so choose, some of the experiments referred to, and for which data are given, could be carried out by the pupils.

Where extra information is needed, it is of a nature which can be found in a wide range of books to be commonly found in schools.

RAINBOWS AND COLOURED LIGHTS

The work is self-contained and no previous knowledge of colour is required. The work could summarise experiments already carried out and the questions be used as test items or homework. This could be used by a reasonably able pupil who has been absent and missed this element of a topic on light to catch up on some of the work missed.

SLIDE PROJECTORS

Basic work on light needs to have been done. Knowledge of the way that convex and concave lenses function is necessary. Knowledge and an understanding of light travelling in straight lines is required.

LIGHT IN OUR EYES

A self-contained package for more able pupils on how a human eye functions. If a three-dimensional model of the eye were available, it would make the work easier to follow.

MIRROR, MIRROR ON THE WALL

Experimental investigations on reflection with flat mirrors need to have been done. Lateral inversion needs to have been experienced and there needs to be an understanding of what an image is.

KEEPING AN IMAGE

Practical experience of how a convex lens functions is necessary. A pinhole camera needs to have been built and used if this piece of work is to be be made maximum use of. Could be used for homework with more able pupils.

EYESIGHT PROBLEMS

Previous knowledge required includes: how the human eye functions and how convex and concave lenses function. Could be used as a cover lesson or for homework.

LIGHT LAW

This could be used to test pupils' degree of understanding of the first law of reflection. An experimental investigation must have been carried out to discover that the angles of incidence and reflection are equal. Experimental work on the effect of curved mirrors needs to have been carried out in order for pupils to be able to give an answer to question 5.

BACK-TO-FRONT REFLECTION

This piece of work can be available either before or instead of more formal experimental work but a flat mirror should then be available. No previous knowledge is essential. Some basic analysis of data is involved.

ALL DONE WITH MIRRORS!

This is a simpler piece of work relating to the first law of reflection and the use and function of convex and concave mirrors. The practical element of this work involves the construction of a periscope. Pieces of thin card 25x40cm are required, together with glue or tape. Two plastic or aluminised card mirrors are required for each periscope.

© 1991 Folens Limited This page may be photocopied for classroom use only

Teachers' Notes

MOVING PICTURES

Previous knowledge required includes an understanding of the basic function of convex lenses. The construction of a 'flick' book and a spinning double-sided picture both help to explain the meaning of the term 'persistence of vision' and thus promote a greater understanding of how the movie projector works.

WAVES ALL AROUND

This could be used as a piece of written research to introduce the electromagnetic spectrum. Previous experience needs to include work on wave motion relating to light and sound. At a more basic level, the piece of work can be used to give some practice in the extraction of data/information from different forms (charts and the written word).

HEAR EAR!

A self-contained piece of work to give pupils an understanding of how the human ear works.

SOUND SURVEY

Pupils need to have used a decibel meter and have an understanding of what 'loudness' means. Data analysis and graphical construction skills are both developed. Could be used to reinforce work on sound level measurement and sound pollution.

NOISE OR MUSIC?

Previous knowledge and experience of wave motion is required. Data analysis is involved, together with graphical construction. Practical experience of the use of a tuning fork makes the work easier to follow. This could be used within a lesson to test understanding of work already covered or can be given as homework.

SPEED OF SOUND

No previous knowledge is required. This activity can be used to introduce experimental work. It involves data-handling and analysis. Pupils need to be able to calculate an average and handle the division of decimals.

HISTORY OF SPACE FLIGHT

No previous knowledge required. Extraction and reorganisation of information is involved.

MOON MATTERS

Understanding of the meaning of gravitational pull and of temperature scales is required. Can be used to reinforce work done on studying the Moon. Can also be linked to observational homework or as part of a school based topic.

TWINKLE, TWINKLE LITTLE STAR

Understanding of what a fuel is and of the meaning of gravitational pull is required. Can be used as a cover lesson or for homework.

SEEING STARS!

Some understanding of temperature scales, radiant energy and the electromagnetic spectrum is required. An introduction to the nature of stars.

OUR SOLAR SYSTEM

No previous knowledge required. Pupils extract and reorganise data. Some skill in scale drawing is needed in order to be able to complete Task 2. Can be used as a self-contained lesson or as a homework.

© 1991 Folens Limited   This page may be photocopied for classroom use only